NEW AUDITION SCENES AND MONOLOGS FROM CONTEMPORARY PLAYWRIGHTS

The best new cuttings from around the world

edited by **Roger Ellis**

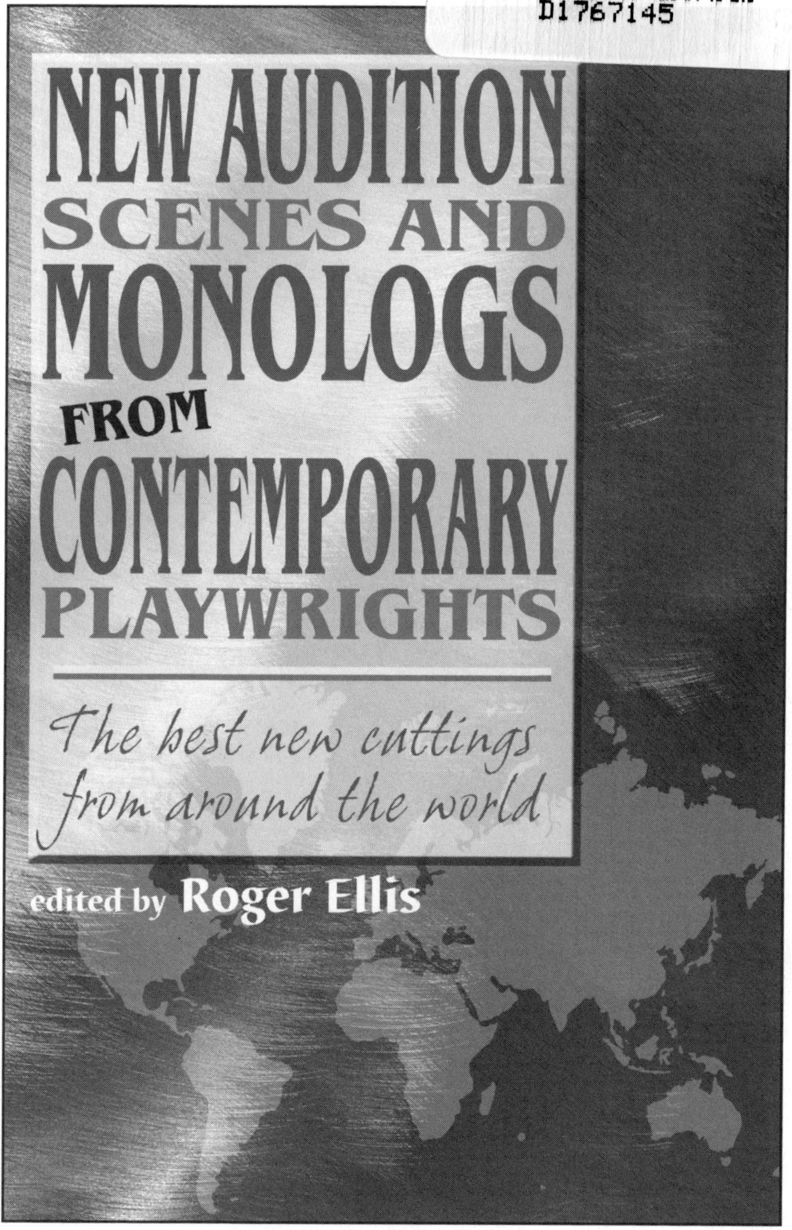

MERIWETHER PUBLISHING LTD.
Colorado Springs, Colorado

Meriwether Publishing Ltd., Publisher
PO Box 7710
Colorado Springs, CO 80933-7710

Associate editor: Theodore O. Zapel
Cover design: Jan Melvin

© Copyright MMV Meriwether Publishing Ltd.
Printed in the United States of America
First Edition

All rights reserved. No part of this publication may be reproduced, stored in a retrieval system, or transmitted in any form or by any means, electronic, mechanical, photocopying, recording or otherwise, without permission of the publishers.

CAUTION: Professionals and amateurs are hereby warned that the plays represented in this book are subject to royalty. They are fully protected under the copyright laws of the United States of America and of all countries covered by the International Copyright Union (including the Dominion of Canada) and of all countries covered by the Pan-American Copyright Convention and the Universal Copyright Convention and of all countries with which the United States has reciprocal copyright relations. All rights, including professional, amateur, motion picture, recitation, lecturing, public reading, radio broadcasting, television, video or sound taping, all other forms of mechanical or electronic reproduction, such as information storage and retrieval systems and photocopying, and the rights of translation into foreign languages, are strictly reserved. Particular emphasis is laid upon the question of readings, permission for which must be secured from the author's agent in writing. These plays may not be publicly performed without express written permission from the author or the author's agent. Pages 171-175 constitute an extension of this copyright page.

Library of Congress Cataloging-in-Publication Data

New audition scenes and monologs from contemporary playwrights : the best new cuttings from around the world / edited with an acting introduction by Roger Ellis.-- 1st ed.
   p. cm.
 ISBN 1-56608-105-X -- ISBN 9781566081054
 1. Acting--Auditions. 2. Monologues. 3. Drama--21st century.
 I. Ellis, Roger, 1943 May 18-
   PN2080.N45 2005
   808.82--dc22
                                    2004028495

     1 2 3   05   06   07
        26.00

Contents

Acknowledgments 1

Preface 3

Performance Introduction:
  Presenting Scenes and Monologs 7

Monologs for Men 19

  Michael – *Reliable Junk* by Ric Averill 21

  Lewis – *Pancake Tuesday* by Lindsay Price 23

  Victor – *Victor* by Ric Averill 25

  Grant – *Reconciliation* by Cary Pepper 27

  Peter – *I'd Know You Anywhere* by Dori Appel 29

  Hopkinson – *Went Down to the Crossroads*
    by Philip Goulding 32

  Man – *I Saw a Woman Murdered the Other Day*
    by William Borden 34

Monologs for Women 37

  Alissa – "Blind Date" by Ann Roth,
    from ***The Blueberry Café*** by Women At Play 39

  Sleeping Beauty – *Fair(l)y (S)tale* by Amanda Kellock 42

  Snow White – *Fair(l)y (S)tale* by Amanda Kellock 44

  Woman – *In the Laundromat* by William Borden 45

  Mabie – *Red Frogs* by Ruth Margraff 47

  Valdetta – *Women Behind the Walls*
    by Claire Braz-Valentine 49

Scenes for Men 51

  Theseus and Daedalus – *The Minotaur*
    by Neil Duffield 53

    Daedalus and Apollo – *The Minotaur*
        by Neil Duffield 57

    Boy and Stevie – *The Trees They
    Grow So High* by Tony Powell 59

    Boy and Stevie – *The Trees They
    Grow So High* by Tony Powell 61

    Steven and Morgan – *Surfing, Carmarthen Bay*
        by Roger Williams 65

    Steve and Edgar – *Wait Wait Bo Bait* by Lindsay Price 70

    Kyle and J.T. – *Another Way Out* by Max Bush 72

Scenes for Women 77

    Sue Ellen and Kara – *Looking Through You*
        by Max Bush 79

    Paula and Sandy – *Markers* by Shirley King 81

    Ruthie and Imogene – "Distended Ear Lobes"
    by Katherine Burkman, from *Imaging Imogene*
    by Women At Play 88

    Valdetta and Nicki – *Women Behind the Walls*
        by Claire Braz-Valentine 92

    Caroline and Veronica – *Two Loves and a Creature*
        by Gustavo Ott 95

Scenes for Men and Women 99

    Leanne, Luke, and Danny – *Guides* by Josh Overton 101

    Abe and Sabra – *How His Bride Came to Abraham*
        by Karen Sunde 106

    Tiffany, Charlie, and Marcia – *Blue Girl*
        by Deborah Aita 111

    Lucy and Will – "Competition" by Elizabeth Nash,
    from *It's Academic* by Women At Play 116

    Ron, Kathryn, and Teresa – *Can't Believe It*
        by R.N. Sandberg 119

    Jake and Anna – *Halls of Horror* by Josh Overton 122

  Daniel and Victoria — *Your Molotov Kisses*
   by Gustavo Ott 125

  Kilobyte, Daisy, and Tarwater — *About Face*
   by Noëlle Janaczewska... 132

  Ms. Gibbons and Spike — *Tagged* by Susan Battye 135

  Young Man and Admissions Clerk —
   No Pain, No Gain by Susan Battye 139

Extended Monologs for Men 143

  Bruce — "On Guard" by Marilyn Rofsky, from
   She of the Lovely Ankle by Women At Play 145

  Sam — "Sam" by Katherine Burkman, from
   She of the Lovely Ankle by Women At Play 148

  Bob — *bobrauschenbergamerica* by Charles L. Mee 151

Extended Monologs for Women 155

  Joanie — *Saints and Angels* by Shirley King 157

  Raleigh — *Audition* by Cary Pepper 162

  Dark Lady — *Terrestrial and Without Imagination*
   by Luiza Carol 166

Credits 171

About the Editor... 177

Acknowledgments

Among the many individuals and organizations who lent me their assistance with this book, special recognition should be given to Grand Valley State University, which provided me with the much-needed funding and release time from teaching and directing in order to compile and prepare the material. I'm also grateful for the continued support of my editor, Ted Zapel, at Meriwether Publishing.

In addition to the people and groups too numerous to mention who have spread the word about my call for scripts for this anthology, I'd like to thank the following individuals and international organizations, which have been instrumental in publicizing my efforts: Association Internationale du Théâtre Amateur/International Amateur Theatre Association (AITA/IATA); American Association for Theatre in Education (AATE); the Australian Script Centre; United States Center for the International Association of Theatre for Children and Young People (ASSITEJ/USA); Women Playwrights International (Australia); Theatre Playwrights Development Collective (Canada); Priscilla Yates of the Australian Writers Guild; Irish Centre of AITA/IATA; Council of Drama in Education (Canada); Australian Capital Territory Drama Association (ACTDA); North European Amateur Theatre Alliance AITA/IATA (NEATA); Replay Productions (Ireland); Gustavo Ott of the South American Regional Alliance AITA/IATA (SARA); and Aled Rhys-Jones of the Drama Association of Wales. Last but not least I owe a debt of gratitude I can never repay to all of the actors and audiences whose performances and responses enabled me to recognize the power and the grace, the subtlety and theatricality of the scenes and monologs contained in this anthology.

Preface

Overview of the Collection

This anthology contains over forty monologs and scenes from the work of contemporary playwrights, selected for use by young students and actors age twelve to twenty-four years old. The material is appropriate for all audiences in terms of language and situations, and the selections vary in length from one to two minutes to approximately nine to ten minutes in order to offer a range of challenges for students who are just beginning to find their voice in theatre. The anthology is designed as a resource text for general reading, competitive auditions, forensics activities, playwriting exercises, literary editing, oral interpretation classes, acting studio exercises, and similar applications.

One of this book's noteworthy features is that it can open doors to many writers who are not widely known within the international performance community. I've relied upon writers' organizations, international drama festivals, new plays programs at established theatres, and Internet-based playwrights' organizations worldwide in order to publicize my call for scripts. Through these, I've succeeded in tapping numerous plays from around the globe that are fresh and exciting. All the excerpts here are fascinating cultural documents that should appeal to students of all ages.

The international flavor of this collection is also noteworthy because it offers some unusual challenges to students or actors from different English-speaking societies. For example, is the piece best presented with or without a dialect? Can one understand the issue at hand without doing research? What does need to be researched about the socio-cultural context or the word usage? And what research methods and skills are needed in order to unleash the full potential of the monologs or scenes?

Readers should note at the outset that with few exceptions, all of the pieces in this collection are taken from unpublished plays. Thus, while the anthology is "fresh," it also discourages students from relying upon the already-existing literary or dramatic context of the selections. This intentional limitation seeks to stimulate the student's imaginative resources by urging him or her to supply original background information, given circumstances, character motivation, biographical details and the like for interpreting the extracts. A brief introduction precedes each selection in order to highlight some key features and point the student in the right direction. But I hope that the material — "isolated" from the complete script in this way — will encourage students to "think outside the box" of given plays and stories in order to improvise and discover their own unique interpretations.

In some situations it may be desirable, of course, to obtain the full script of a play, and I've tried to supply accurate information in the credits section of this anthology to help students and their coaches contact the authors or their agents directly. In fact, most of these authors would love to have you read their complete work because public exposure is a vital elixir for their careers and often leads to full stagings of their plays. But realistically, the contact information at the end of the text may quickly become out of date as writers change their addresses or their agents, and for writers living abroad, the task of contacting them may be daunting. In any case, I feel the value of a fresh collection of very recent and infrequently seen excerpts from contemporary international plays outweighs the drawback of limited accessibility to the full, published script.

Criteria for Selecting Material

One of the basic criteria governing my choice of scenes and monologs has been the requirement that all the pieces be taken from plays that have been produced in some form: full productions, staged readings, workshops, etc. I feel this is the only way for writers to develop speakable dialog, compelling character traits, dramatic development, and so forth. Unlike the solitary working methods of poets, novelists, and authors in literary forms, playwrights need to forge their dramas in the crucible of actor-audience interaction. They need to ensure that their words communicate vividly, vitally, and immediately to spectators across the footlights and score an impact on the audience. After all, plays are designed to be spoken, not read. Not all writing, however colorful, functions theatrically in this way, but I feel that all the material in this collection does.

I've also been keenly concerned with the suitability of this material for educational purposes. Hence, I've included some brief tips in the book's introduction on how to rehearse and present the selections either for forensics interpretation and training or for acting classes, auditions, and the like. I've also tried to select only those pieces with characters able to be played by young actors between twelve and twenty-four years of age. This ensures that the scenes and monologs will present opportunities for students to "use themselves" and closely identify with the material they're presenting.

Third, I've tried to focus on plays containing themes of interest to this age group. Some of the dramas, such as *Blue Girl* by Deborah Aita (New Zealand), *Halls Of Horror* by Josh Overton (U.S.A.), and *The Minotaur* by Neil Duffield (United Kingdom) have been specifically written for young audiences. However, readers will soon discover that the majority of these plays have been written for general audiences, although the selections here contain themes or characters especially appropriate for younger students to examine and develop. As a stage director, I've always felt the plays that best entertain and serve young audiences are those that work with general audiences as well.

Finally, the need to balance the treatment of gender, ethnic, and racial diversity in the collection has also governed my choice of material to some extent. For example, the number of male and female writers represented in this collection, as well as the number of male and female roles, is roughly equal. In the category of ethnic diversity, I've sought to include characters from Arabic, African-American, Jewish, and other racial or ethnic backgrounds in order to reflect the increasing cultural pluralism both in our schools and in society at large. Where necessary, I've indicated specific gender and ethnic features of the characters in the acting prefaces to the various selections.

My hope in doing all this has been that the book will serve the special needs of teachers and students in middle school, high school, and university classrooms as a reading text, a class performance text, and a competition resource.

Editorial Changes

I haven't modified any of the pieces, except to remove them from the context of the entire play, number the lines for reference, and preface each with brief suggestions on performance approaches. All the extracts have been reviewed and approved by the authors, and in most cases the authors have also had a hand in shaping the prefatory comments preceding each extract.

One of the collection's most interesting features is the variety in length of the selections. Longer pieces offer teachers the opportunity to discuss editing methods, and they challenge students to explore ways of condensing and focusing the text.

Coaches and students preparing for competitive auditions — scholarships, casting, forensics competitions, etc. — might therefore find value in learning how to trim and compress their selections to a shorter length. And at least five or six of the selections can stand on their own as short one-acts.

Students and their coaches should also remember that the printed length of a monolog or scene is never a good indication of its performance length, which always depends on the number of heartbeats — not the number of words. All the selections must therefore be studied and presented aloud, if only to judge their length and the emotional power they contain.

A Reminder about Intellectual Property

In all the anthologies I edit, I feel compelled to remind readers that the work in the collection is intended *only* for studio exercises or for reading. When it comes to performing it, producing it in public readings, or adapting it in any way via the electronic media for other audiences — educational, amateur, or professional — permission *must* be obtained and royalties paid to the agent or author.

Perhaps this "caution" needs to be frequently restated in this age of the Internet, where so much is available online or otherwise reproducible at little or no charge. Readers must remind themselves that plays — like other unique, cultural artifacts — are not equivalent to the cheapened bytes and "factoids" we slug through and manipulate by the thousands every day. They are the intellectual property of human beings who have spent many years earning, and who therefore deserve, proper acknowledgment and compensation for producing and distributing them to the public.

Bear in mind that in this book I'm attempting to highlight and promote the work of a handful of uniquely talented and very highly motivated artists whose worth, importance, and cultural value in our society is already deeply discounted, frequently ridiculed, and even despised. Their plays are their honest work, their "products." Pay for them. If you wish to perform any of these monologs in public, credits appear at the end of this volume; call or write for permission. These artists are not unreasonable in what they expect from us.

Performance Introduction: Presenting Scenes and Monologs

Reading Aloud

To get yourself in shape to present scenes or monologs, and to keep your presentations fresh, *the single most valuable exercise you can do is to read aloud daily for fifteen to thirty minutes.* Reading aloud is easy to accomplish if you just set aside the time. The activity requires no audience, no special materials, no special place. You can read anything aloud, anywhere, anytime, and it will do wonders to help improve your performance skills and keep them up to speed.

You don't need to use just dramatic material for this. Frequently the opposite of "dramatic" material is fun and challenging. Try reading a cookbook, a computer manual, a comic book, or a children's story with animation, suspense, excitement, surprise, and "drama"! Of course, dramatic scripts work especially well because they're written in order to be spoken, and accomplished writers (like the ones in this anthology) have filled their monologs and scenes with all those "dramatic" elements that are so exciting to present: conflict, change, struggle, relationships, self-discoveries, surprises, and so forth.

You need to develop several skills by reading aloud daily. Most of all, you need to develop **fluency**, the ability to read out loud off the page smoothly and confidently. Although most people cannot do this very well, it is a fundamental skill that all presenters need to master. Whether you're giving a speech, preparing to compete in forensics interpretation, perform cold readings at an audition, or act a role script-in-hand at a staged reading, fluency is an absolute requirement.

Daily practice will help you eliminate vocalized pauses ("uhhmm"); nonfluent repetitions ("y'know" or "like"); hesitations and stumbling over words and phrases; or panicky, rushed delivery on account of stage fright. Daily practice will also make you feel more comfortable with your own voice, and it will strengthen the vocal muscles that live performance requires. But you have to keep at it. If you cannot read with fluency after one to two weeks of practice, then it is probably best for you to double your daily practice time.

The second skill you'll develop by reading aloud every day is **vocal expressiveness**. You should find after a couple of weeks that you're displaying more *inflection and melody* (pitch range) in your voice, that you're using more variety of *volume*, that your *articulation and clarity* are improving, and that your *pace of delivery* and your *ability to gather and phrase words* are becoming much more flexible, controlled, and expressive. Incidentally, it helps to rehearse your pieces with a tape recorder so that you can listen to yourself as you work on all these skills and keep a record of your progress week by week.

Finally, reading aloud every day will help you develop the skills of looking up from the page as you read and of moving freely and expressively within the space. Bear in mind that the aim of oral interpretation is not to get the words "right," but to express them vividly, fully, and meaningfully. Remember, too, that all dramatic writings — including single-character monologs — *are written to be spoken to someone,* either real or imagined. You must make eye contact with this other character — real or imagined — just as you do in everyday life when speaking with others. And you must embody the sense of your words as fully as possible by expressing your thoughts with gestures and movements.

These are very difficult and challenging tasks for students. For example, many actors try to conceal their stage fright by "hiding behind the script" as they perform. I notice people glued to their scripts all the time in auditions and it drives me crazy, as though the words they're reading were more important than the relationships they're portraying. I don't cast actors because of how well they read; I want to see them create chemistry up there. And you can't begin to use your imagination, create a relationship, or "act" until you've freed yourself from dependency on the page. It's just too distracting.

So as you practice reading aloud every day, work toward the point where you can "scan" a few words ahead and then look up from the page as you speak. Also master the skill of holding your text in one hand, keeping your place on the page with your thumb, while you use your other hand for gesturing. The more you rehearse your monolog or scene in this way, the more familiar you'll become with the text, and the easier it will be to look up from the page, gesture, and move as you speak. And very soon you will have it memorized anyway!

Preparing Monologs and Scenes
Exploring Text and Subtext

The first step you must take to prepare your monolog or scene is to **paraphrase it**. A paraphrase is a rewording of the original text in your own language — your everyday idioms, speech patterns, word choices, etc. — in order to capture a sense of what is actually being said and to identify how and why the character's rhetoric differs from yours.

The literal meaning of what is being said is the *denotation*, and you should always refer to a dictionary when encountering words that are unfamiliar to you. The implied or underlying meaning is even more important, and this is called the *connotation*. The connotation of words yield vital clues about the way characters really think and feel, the "subtext" of the monolog. In these two ways, a paraphrase will always alert you to words or phrases you may not have completely understood at first reading.

Do *not* assume that you know what a word means simply "from the context" (i.e., guessing). And don't be lazy. Go to a dictionary and get the pronunciation and the meaning right. There are few things more embarrassing than having to listen to a student who is passionately acting up a storm — and is completely mistaken about the sense of a word, clueless about the underlying meaning of a phrase, or oblivious to the subtext of the speech.

Next, use the paraphrase to help you **personalize the selection**. This means that you must find common ground between you and the character's favorable, as well as unfavorable, aspects. By and large, the extracts contained here were selected because they voice one or more concerns that are commonly shared by young students, so you shouldn't have to reach too far in order to understand and appreciate what is being thought and said.

Look carefully, though, at what these dramatic characters are saying, what they're feeling, and what they're believing. Then look to see whether or not your paraphrase actually captured that. You'll probably find things that you don't share with that character or that you reject in your own personal life. In short, in order to fully exploit the scene or the monolog's potential, you must find some point of contact with *all* the issues, emotions, and values that you (the character) will struggle with and express to your audience.

Paraphrasing is a very important first step, and many students ignore writing it out and comparing it with the original because they assume that the scene or monolog is readily understandable, and of course they're eager to act it out. Remember, though, that you simply cannot present what you don't understand. If you throw away words, ideas, and images that you regard as unimportant, objectionable, or embarrassing to present in public, you'll likely reduce a rich dramatic character to your own everyday personality. In short, you'll just be going through the motions and mouthing the words. Your performance will ring hollow because the text will signal more than you are able to give it.

Playing Relationships

After exploring the material with paraphrase in order to see what's actually contained in it, your next step is to **identify the relationships** that the piece defines. Bear in mind that every bit of acting you will ever do is based upon relationship — not glorious language or spectacular effects or high-energy emotions or anything else. Whether you're presenting an oral interpretation, a staged reading, or a full-blown acting performance, if you fail to create a relationship with another person, you'll seem flat and uninteresting to listeners. We don't go to the theatre or cinema to look at the scenery or listen to the music or get blown away by raging passions and clever effects; we come to identify with the people in the story and the problems they grapple with, and hopefully be moved by that experience.

There are two relationships you must always define for yourself: your relationship with the audience or listeners, and your character's relationship with the vis-à-vis. (Vis-à-vis is an acting term that means the other character to whom you're speaking.) In the first case, you must ask yourself why these ideas are important to communicate. What's in it for the audience? How are they supposed to be moved by these words? What should they feel or experience? And how can you accomplish that? How can you "score that impact" on the auditors or judges or directors?

You can begin by reminding yourself that all acting is communication — a point that most people forget because plays and films and television are often regarded merely as entertainment. Actors tend to forget this, too, in the wake of rehearsing, getting onstage, calming their nerves, enduring the critical gaze of the spectators, performing their scenes or monologs, or even getting through an entire show in a role.

In order to communicate well, you must be personally confident that there is a valuable goal in the monolog or scene. To take someone's mind off their terrible grief for a few moments? To remind them of the common spark of humanity that all of us — including the bad guys and riffraff — share? To throw some new emphasis on the sufferings of rejected lovers? To explore the fear of loneliness? The sadness of isolation? The numbness of alienation? What exactly is important for you to express to your public in this piece? There must have been something or you wouldn't have been attracted to it, right?

If you believe this, if you believe in what you need to accomplish with your interpretation, it will be so much easier for you to perform your piece compellingly, and you'll be much more confident about overcoming the stage fright and jitters that always accompany public presentations. If nothing else, remember that people don't go to the theatre or to films to see ordinary life or experience common emotions. We pay good money to be moved and to get something we just can't find in our everyday lives. So discover what that something is that your piece can do for the listener and make it happen!

The second relationship you need to clearly define for yourself and the audience is your immediate, moment-by-moment relationship with the vis-à-vis. You should begin by assuming that you (the character) would die if you could not speak these things to this particular person at this particular time. You must assume that you have an itch that you've just got to scratch, a problem that you absolutely must resolve — here and now — with this other person who is listening.

Remember that nothing in the theatre is ordinary: Your relationship to your vis-à-vis must be compelling. Only this person can give you what you need, and this person must give it to you now. You need to believe in this commitment as fully as possible in order to "raise the stakes" and generate the energy that the dramatic situation requires. After all, if you don't believe that the words you're speaking are important enough for your vis-à-vis to listen to, then your audience certainly won't listen either.

When you're rehearsing a scene, of course, your vis-à-vis will be your acting partner(s) playing the other character(s); but with a monolog you'll have to *imagine* this other character in the scene with you. In some of the monologs here you'll find the vis-à-vis clearly defined for you: a lover, a brother, a parent, someone concrete. In most of them, however, you must invent the vis-à-vis for yourself. This is one of the most enjoyable challenges an actor will face, because it allows you to choose any imaginary listener you want. You are in control!

In either case — whether the vis-à-vis is defined or not — *you should try to imagine that listener as concretely and vividly as possible.* Choose details and people from your personal life that will give you the most vivid feedback. Someone who argues relentlessly with you, someone who throws him- or herself passionately into your arms, abuses you, cheers you on, frustrates you with questions, mocks you — these are the best vis-à-vis. You need someone who *disturbs* you as you deliver the speech or tell the story. The more you believe in your imaginary listener, the more you'll energize your presentation, and the less stage fright will assail you.

When rehearsing the piece, in fact, you should visualize that imaginary listener's actual physical responses to what you're saying in order to strengthen your attempt to clarify, emphasize, persuade, and win them over with the speech. Is that listener objecting? About to interrupt? Starting to leave and reject what you're saying? Laughing at your words? Crying at what you're saying? What, exactly? Play with these imaginary responses as you prepare your monolog and use the words of the speech to overcome the objections of your vis-à-vis and get what you want.

Fight to communicate and score an impact on your listener and you will discover your performance taking on a whole new energy, a whole new life that will compel the attention of the auditor, the director, or the judge.

Playing Goals

In addition to making the vis-à-vis as concrete and active as possible, you also need to **identify what it is that you're fighting for in the scene.** If the monolog or scene doesn't exactly tell you what it is you want from the other character, you'll have to invent it. But whether your goal is identified by the playwright or not, you should make it as detailed and as specific as possible in order to play it effectively in the scene. Actors sometimes refer to this target as the "goal," "objective," or "intention" in the scene.

First of all, when beginning to determine what your character is fighting for, remember that in real life no one simply hands us whatever we want. We must demand strongly, insistently, forcefully in order to get what's really important for us in our lives. It is this "fighting for" that lends urgency and especially sharp focus to your acting. Combined with a concrete vis-à-vis, this active goal for your speech will add up to a performance that is rich with energy and loaded with interest for your listeners.

Second, take a tip from professional actors who often identify this "fighting for" in terms of a strong, active, infinitive verb. You want *to guilt* him in the monolog, *to mock* her, *to drive* him to tears, *to seduce* her kind feelings, *to demand* that he apologize, *to trick* her out of money, to get her *to fall desperately* in love with you, and so forth. Many beginning actors fail to choose vivid actions like these to play, feeling that their "instincts" and the words alone will "carry them through" the performance. This attitude can be the kiss of death because when you've failed to stress, moment-by-moment, the specific needs that underlie your character's words, the scene and the relationship seem limp and flaccid to the listeners.

Finally, remember that in real life what we want from other people is rarely single-minded or simple. Our goals, our "fighting fors" are often multiple and can be very complex. So, too, in the monologs and scenes that follow, discover how each character's objectives change and develop as he or she continues speaking. No single "fighting for" will get you through the entire speech. You can't play the entire scene just angrily or whiningly or fearfully or ecstatically or anything else. You must always end up in a different emotional or spiritual place than where you began. So look for the emotional colors along that spiritual journey of the speech or scene. Something *must* happen, some change *must* occur.

Playing the Events

This brings us to the next step you must take: **eventing the script.** The great American acting teacher Michael Shurtleff was fond of using this phrase. What it means is that *you must divide the monolog or scene into a beginning, a middle, and an end; and that you must find in each of those the subsections or "beats" where "events"—physical or psychological — happen to you.* Where do your thoughts change? Where do your verbal tactics change? Have you discovered something new as you speak? Do the stage directions indicate that you physically do some things at certain points? Does that lead you in new directions? And how does all this bring you to the final point you want to reach in the monolog or scene? In short, what is the *pattern of actions* that takes you from point A to point Z? Another great American acting teacher, Uta Hagen, once remarked that the pattern of actions you choose to play in your monolog or scene is the single most effective thing you can do to improve your acting.

When you rehearse your piece, you must strive to *play each of these beats separately and distinctly in order to "mark" the progress or development of your thoughts in the piece.* If you do this, you'll find sudden *contrasts* where one beat changes to another as the result of some new idea. You'll stumble upon those highly dramatic moments of *discovery* as you speak. You'll also make surprising *connections and transitions* from one idea or emotional state to another. And the *pace* of your delivery and *emotional moods* will vary, propelling the monolog forward and engaging your listeners' attention moment-by-moment as you act it out.

Remember, you must never end a monolog at the same emotional or spiritual place that you began. Play the selection so that important events happen to the character en route, in order to make us believe that his or her world has changed dramatically by the time the scene has finished.

Rehearsing Monologs and Scenes

Once you've completed the preparatory work discussed above, you're ready to rehearse. Your first step in rehearsal is to **score your script.** This means marking up your script, treating it as a musical "score" that you'll use in performance. You'll need at least three copies for this: two "rough drafts" and a "final" version. When you get copies, try to get them larger than the printed text you ordinarily find in published playscripts, and always mark your script in pencil because you're going to change your mind often as rehearsals proceed.

Actors use a variety of notations to score their scripts. Probably the most familiar is using highlighter pens to identify words or phrases you want to vocally emphasize. But there are other things besides emphasis that are important to you. For one thing, you should always draw a line across the page to separate the beats in a monolog and reinforce their distinctness in your mind as you memorize and rehearse. And penciled notations in the margin beside each beat keep you focused on the infinitive phrase that tells you what you're fighting for there. Actors also frequently draw a diagonal line between words, phrases, or sentences to indicate where pauses should occur. An asterisk or a circled word connected by a line to a margin note can remind you of physical actions or staging movements that should be made at that point. Some other marginal notations I like to make in scripts include wavy lines that suggest changes in tempo or pace and small arrows indicating rising or falling inflections in vocal delivery.

Don't overdo this, of course, because you won't follow every mark on the page when you eventually go onstage. But physically scoring the script in this way helps you to identify and set the technical aspects of the monolog or scene in your mind prior to memorizing it or presenting it script-in-hand. It also helps you to exploit all the literary and dramatic aspects of the writing the author has given you. You'll be surprised what you turn up. And of course, if you're doing a nonmemorized oral interpretation of the monolog, then you'll want to gradually reduce the notations to just those that you find are absolutely essential, and that you can comfortably and effectively follow as you read it publicly.

Next you must **memorize the piece,** or key sections of it, for an effective presentation. Of course, for a theatrical audition and many class assignments the piece must be entirely memorized. Only when you free yourself from reading the text off a page and can speak it confidently and naturally will you be able to identify psycho-physically with the character. Even with nonmemorized presentations, as with any public address, you should always memorize the key sections that require maximum eye contact, maximum emotional intensity, maximum belief in and commitment to the dramatic situation. Memorization also frees you to physicalize the actions in the text with hand and arm gestures, blocking movements in the space, and changes in posture and body position.

Allow yourself plenty of time for **staged rehearsals.** These should serve several purposes. For one thing, get used to the sound of your voice, and work to connect voice and movement in order to gain a "natural" feel for living the life of the character. Also you must always rehearse the monolog aloud. Running it over in your head again and again will do absolutely nothing for you and will only serve to increase your anxiety and insecurity. Most of all, avoid treating the rehearsal as an attempt to finally "get it memorized" — to get it all set and fixed and consistent. Instead, use much of your rehearsal time to discover new things to do in the monolog, both vocally and physically.

Remember that there will be plenty of time later on to drill yourself for sheer memorization and repeatability, so you must strive to *keep it fresh and spontaneous.* You can just bet that you'll be speaking it aloud to yourself in the shower, in the car, while you're "waiting in the wings," or whatever. People will likely think you're going crazy talking to yourself so much. So always use rehearsals to uncover new possibilities you may have overlooked, to exploit each and every phrase for maximum dramatic potential, and to "open up" the text by experimenting with surprising and original choices for physical actions and vocal power.

Your next step in preparation is to **discover physical movements or blocking** that will enhance the selection. In general, young actors tend to make *too many* movements: random paces and crosses or nervous hand and arm gestures that only serve to muddy the dramatic action taking place or to confuse the spectator. Rehearsals are often valuable, therefore, for *reducing* the movements that may have cluttered the enactment. Remember that movements should only underscore what is happening in the text; never move just for the sake of moving, or because you feel you've been standing in one place for too long. What matters are the heartbeats expressed in the monolog, not how much visual variety and excitement you're giving the onlookers.

To devise effective movements for yourself, you should begin with the stage directions offered by the playwright. While it's not essential for you to perform them, they certainly do give a good indication of where the monolog *might* be enhanced by a certain kind of gesture or posture or movement. Next, you want to be certain to place your imaginary vis-à-vis downstage of you so that you can be fully visible from the front, where the listeners will see you. You can then seek to physicalize (emphasize and set off) each beat of the monolog or scene by changing your stage position in relation to your vis-à-vis: circling him or her, approaching or withdrawing, turning away, threatening, pleading, etc. Some of the extracts in this book even contain sections where characters speak directly "out" (into the auditorium), such as at moments of reflection or recollection. At these points you can move downstage to do just that — although never look straight at a director, auditor, or forensics judge in a competitive performance situation.

One type of movement that you should always avoid is pantomiming objects such as furniture or hand properties. This always "breaks the illusion" you're seeking to create and reminds the audience that you're "acting." Limit yourself to a simple table and a couple of chairs, and devise ways to do without any other props or furniture that you might be tempted to add or that are indicated in the text. I've tried to be careful in selecting material for this book, and none of the selections absolutely *requires* physical objects for its presentation.

On the other hand, having a small physical prop in your hand can be very reassuring when it comes to mastering stage fright. For example, a book or magazine or eyeglasses — particularly when they are suggested in the script or can be made to seem natural and appropriate in the situation — might sometimes help the presentation. But in most cases, larger properties, such as costumes or special furniture, are unnecessary. What the spectators want to see is you, not the furniture.

You can also help yourself in the rehearsal process if you **find people to listen to you** once you've shaped the piece into a presentable form. Friends are always good for this because they give you a chance to accustom yourself to eyeballs actually looking at you while you perform it. They can also spot obvious mannerisms you may have overlooked because you're so close to the material and you've been rehearsing it so much. For example, are you unconsciously using the same hand gestures over and over again? (Have them plug their ears and just watch you.) Or does your voice fall into repetitious vocal patterns the longer you continue? (Have them close their eyes and just listen to you.) Friends can also pass along some ideas that you might not have considered: possibilities for movement or different interpretations of lines or phrases.

A second valuable rehearsal approach is to **find a teacher or director** who can coach you as a critical listener. This is absolutely essential with competitive performances of any kind. A dramatic coach will be more objective than your friends in assessing whether or not the enactment "shows you at your best," or in suggesting where you need to push yourself more to derive the maximum dramatic value from a phrase or section of the speech.

Dramatic coaches are also valuable critics for all those "technical" things that tend to escape us when we self-rehearse. Are you projecting well at all points in the scene? Are you exceeding the time limits? Can *every word* be heard, or are you slurring word endings and "throwing away" the first couple words at the beginning or the end of a line? Do the movements enhance or muddy the sense of the speech? Are you looking at the floor sometimes as you act? Is the pacing monotonous, are the transitions sharp, and are the emotional colors expressed with sufficient variety?

Finally, **don't concentrate on "getting it right"** because there is no one "right" way to do it, any more than there is only one "right" Hamlet or one "right" Ophelia. Acting is not supposed to be like figuring an algebra equation. Hamlet and Ophelia are only the actors presently playing the roles, with their own singularities, original choices, emotional responses, and personal interpretations. Be brave, take risks, and make *your* own original choices that will enliven the selections that follow.

I hope that all these suggestions will help you in preparing these pieces, and perhaps you have other helpful techniques of your own that I haven't covered here. Above all, remember that dramatic literature is not something that can be completely apprehended at a single sitting. It's designed to be acted, to be rehearsed, to be explored again and again, and to be shaped — to be fleshed out — by the unique, original choices that each and every actor brings to it.

Monologs for Men

Reliable Junk
by Ric Averill

Michael — 20s   Serious

Michael has been a skeptic about the flying machine invented by the eccentric junk-inventor Harvey Scheetz. He is resentful of Harvey for thinking he could do anything about cancer, especially since Michael's own grandfather has been diagnosed with the disease. In this scene, Michael comes to console Harvey after the death of Turk, the young girl whose life Harvey prolonged with his inventions. The scene offers good suggestions for physical actions while the actor, as Michael, struggles for words to console Harvey and explain his own tangled feelings in the situation.

MICHAEL: Hello, Harvey? *(HARVEY doesn't turn. He continues to work.)* **Harvey, it's me, Michael.** *(HARVEY still doesn't look around.)* **Hey, Mister Curtis told me you'd be here.** *(Still nothing. MICHAEL is uncomfortable.)* **Been kind of rough these past few weeks, huh? I thought you might want to look at these pictures.** *(Holds out pictures, still nothing.)* **I'm going to Ohio to visit my Grandpa this weekend. Maybe I should take the flying machine, huh? The pictures are really incredible.** *(Still nothing.)* **Yeah, well, okay. Mister Curtis said you're taking some medicine and you might not want company but I had to come. I'll see you when I get back, okay?** *(He starts to leave but turns back.)* **I'm sorry about ... I just wanted to tell you ... to tell you I'm sorry I was so, you know, so mean about your inventions and stuff, at first. Making fun and stuff, it's just ... I'm sorry about Turk and I ...** *(He stops, thinking*

Harvey is not listening at all, shakes his head, gets ready to leave, turns back.) **Did you really think you could, you know, keep her ... alive, I mean . ... There was nothing you could do.** *(HARVEY starts to break down, then stiffens and turns away.)* **It's not your fault. You don't think it's your fault, do you?** *(MICHAEL pauses, leans down.)* **At the funeral, they talked about you, about how much you loved her and how much you meant to her. Mister Curtis said she was still flying, if it helps.** *(No response. MICHAEL waits a moment.)* **You did what you could, Harvey. Didn't you do everything you could?** *(MICHAEL suddenly thinks of something, walks back to Harvey and sets the pictures down.)* **Maybe you'll want to look at these pictures sometime. I sent a couple to the newspaper.** *(HARVEY looks up.)* **I made up a card for myself, too. Here ...** *(Offers a card to HARVEY who doesn't take it. MICHAEL reads it out loud.)* **Michael Ahrens, Photographer, Weird Investigator. Certifiable Lunatic.** *(MICHAEL puts his hand on HARVEY's shoulder, just as MISTER CURTIS comforted him.)* **Harvey, I'm sorry. I wish it could be three weeks ago for both of us. I really do. I wish I could bring Grandpa here and show him your stuff.** *(Pause.)* **I'll see you when I get back from Ohio, okay?** *(MICHAEL walks slowly out of the room.)*

Pancake Tuesday
by Lindsay Price

Lewis — 20s   Comic

    Lewis is a gentle accountant who's always trying to please everyone. Right now he's standing on the ledge of a building preparing to jump after his company has gone belly up. He's speaking to his business partner and friend, Foster. After a lifetime of following Foster's lead, Lewis finally tells Foster what he really thinks.

LEWIS: That's the trouble with you, Foster. Nothing is ever good enough. Ed's clothes aren't good enough. Our business isn't good enough. We had a nice little small dinky stupid company, Foster. Design a few websites. Make some money. But that wasn't good enough. We had to go big, bigger, best. F.L.E. Advertising Incorporated. More office space. More computers. More employees. We have a VP of business strategy. When did that happen? Then when we were big, that wasn't good enough. Gotta go side line. Gotta get into stuff on the side. Keep the balls in the air. You've been like this ever since you were a kid. Ever since, ever since ... *(He takes a deep breath in and blows it out as if recalling a painful memory.)* We had a very nice lemonade stand. A perfectly fine, make some pocket money, keeping busy during the summer lemonade stand. That wasn't good enough. It had to be extra special super duper special ingredient lemonade. Every kid on Garden Street ended up vomiting out of windows. You couldn't walk down the street without dodging a spray of spew. We were banned for life from ever having a lemonade stand. Banned for life! Do you know what that feels like? Some kids got sick? Foster, you are just a ... you're just a ... a ... a ... *(He takes another deep breath as if he's about to say something he's never said before.)* **You are a mean man!** You're a mean man. You're bossy, a bore, a pain to live with and work for. You have no sense of humour, no fun, no joie de vivre, no inner child. You're the most hateful human being I've ever met and I believe one hundred percent you're the reason we went down the tubes. You're a big bully and you bully everyone into thinking your way. But you make bad decisions, Foster. Bad, bad, bad. Who gets into on-line marketing when everyone knows it's on the skids? And every one of your stupid side-line ventures was a stinkeroo! Nobody wanted to buy the Bingo dabber holders! No one! You sunk company money into Bingo dabber holders! No wonder we're standing here. No wonder I'm standing here because I went along with it. I go along. Go along Lewis, that's me. I always go along with your stupid ideas 'cause you wouldn't have it any other way and believe you me I am looking forward to seeing your guts spilled out over the sidewalk; fodder for the rats and the pigeons and anyone else who wants 'em! It'll be the sweetest moment of my entire life! Except for the fact that my guts will be lying there beside yours. *(He takes a deep cleansing breath.)* Wow. I feel great. I've wanted to say that for years. I can't believe I've never done it before. I almost came close when you stole Annabel Cleary from me and then told her I had lupus and then dumped her. I almost told you off then. This has been inside me like a boil. A boil on the lining of my stomach, like acid eating away at my intestines. All these years and it was so easy. Wow. I forgive you man. You're the best friend a guy could ever have. *(He takes a deep breath.)* **I can jump off this building with a clear conscience. I'm ready now.**

Victor
by Ric Averill
adapted from *Frankenstein* by Mary Shelley

Victor — 20s Serious

In this retelling of the old story, Victor Frankenstein is kneeling in a graveyard, speaking to his classmates, and expressing his mad vision. He would be dressed as part Goth, part nineteenth-century, in a long black coat, resembling something between an "angry young man" and a "science nerd." The piece reflects the early madness of the egotistical scientist, contemptuous of his teachers and eager to please his admiring peers. At the same time, however, it contains very moving and accurate philosophical observations about the nature of life and consciousness, and it expresses humanity's age-old quest to investigate and bring to light the deepest secrets of nature. Halfway through the monolog Victor picks up a body part lying nearby in the dirt, a disembodied hand.

VICTOR: In the cemetery of dead professors, old brains rot. *(He drops the dirt.)* **In the cemetery of dead professors, new ideas are born.** *(He picks up another handful.)* **In the cemetery of dead professors, old brains rot.** *(Pause.)* **Walden's doing a lecture on reanimation tomorrow, with electricity ... an experiment with a dead mouse. I get to put the poor creature to sleep, but then ... then ... nothing. The dear professor will stop short of anything really challenging. Walden's a frightened old man with one foot already in this graveyard. He'll hook the mouse to electrodes and make it jump, talk about the importance of electricity – but he doesn't understand the possibilities ...**

no, no, he refuses to explore them, refuses to look at the most significant written theories. Magnus, Agrippa, Paracelsus. He forbids their books, ignores their work. *(Imitating the professor:)* "**Mystical obsession is not a topic for discussion in this field of science.**" *(Holds up a dead hand:)* **But what of this hand, this fresh dead hand? Professor — galvanization, alchemy, memory of the soul, the inner spark of life in the tiniest subset of the body — all are connected — maybe mystical, perhaps even magical — and "provable." You'll see. In each element of creation, there is a cosmic memory. This hand has its own knowledge of all that's gone before. We need to find a way to take that knowledge, the wisdom of collective consciousness sleeping in tissue, and bring it into being — so that the human race can progress — at a pace never before thought possible. Imagine the wisest brain, the strongest heart, the most powerful frame, the sharpest eyes and the knowledge of all they've seen. Imagine that, Professor Walden, and watch me, Victor Frankenstein, bring it into being.**

Reconciliation
by Cary Pepper

Grant — 20s   Serious

Grant speaks to his dying older brother, knowing this may be the last time they'll talk. Years ago his brother was turned out of the house and disowned by their parents for confessing his gay feelings to them. Grant, however, remained at home and so his father spoiled him because he was the brother who turned out "normal." Grant realizes why he has grown up so terribly lonely, alienated from his parents and his absent brother, hating his father, his brother, and himself. He now detests the "dirty secret" that in reality denied him a loving brother. The monolog builds steadily from beginning to end, and it challenges the actor to achieve emotional variety so the speech doesn't resemble a long, boring, and angry tirade. In addition to rebellion against his parents, there is great sadness in Grant's words, as well as sympathy, pleading, self-hatred, and confusion as he struggles to piece his life together in what may be his last conversation with his brother.

GRANT: You think this is only about you? You think you're the only one who's been screwed over? You left ... You got out. I stayed ... I stayed in that house, with him ... And their dirty secret you could never talk about, but that they couldn't quite manage to hide. You'd think he'd at least be happy you left. Or happy because I turned out "normal" ... Or happy about *something*, once the secret disappeared ... But no. Maybe he was terrified one day I'd sit him down at the kitchen table and say, "Guess what? Now there are two of us!" Who knew what was going on in his head? But he'd either cut me out, too, or he'd be all over me. So he gives me everything I want ... I don't even have to ask. But half the time it felt like he was trying to buy me off. The other half, thanking me. So I lost you ... and I lost him ... and I lost ... And then you call and tell me you're dying ... And you're not even dying from the right thing! And I come here ... where everything is different ... everywhere I turn I ... I don't know what the hell is going on ... I'm making it up as I go along ... I have to ask people everything about you ... *(He begins to sob.)* All these years ... I'm hating him for what he did to you ... And hating him for what he did to me ... And hating me, for ... And you think this is only about *you!?*

I'd Know You Anywhere
by Dori Appel

Peter — 30s   Seriocomic

Peter, a young man in his early thirties is very sincere, though perhaps slightly mad. He is talking to his wife's mother, Andrea, who has finally tracked him to the aviary at the zoo after his long, mysterious disappearance.

PETER: You're thinking I'm crazy, aren't you — living in the zoo all these months? But you've got to understand, Andrea, I really thought I could learn why it is that some people — like me — have nothing but good fortune, while others — like my brother Percy, who is really a much better person than I am — are constant targets for attack. I came here because I thought that birds might reveal the answer. Think about it: each bird song must have its own vibration, right? So if I could just discover which ones are the harmonious vibrations, and which ones attract trouble ... Don't you see, the aviary is the perfect laboratory! We've got everything here — jolly, light-hearted birds and morose, depressive birds. Excited birds, phlegmatic birds, pondering, reflective birds, and even a few mean, ill-tempered, ornery birds that nothing seems to please. Because in their vibrations and their tiny bird-brains there are all these crucial differences, and I thought those differences might hold the answer. *(Beat.)* But it seems that the answer is ... a mystery. Oh, once in a while you can see that a certain bird has a sweeter nature, or a tougher body — or even better parents. Some parents are really on top of it — bringing back these really fat, terrific worms, patting the kids with their wing-tips. (They do that – very lightly with the little tippy part.) But then there are the other kind, the ones that always get a late start – gotta have a second cup of coffee, read the newspaper. When they finally get moving, they bring back these skinny, anemic-looking worms and just toss 'em at the nest. If they go to pat the babies, it always ends up that they kind of bop 'em by mistake. *(Beat.)* But that doesn't tell you how the kids will turn out, any more than it does with people. Percy and I had the same parents, didn't we? And besides that we're *twins!* What I'm saying is, it's unfathomable – who sings and rejoices, who goes attacking and marauding, and who suddenly topples off a tree branch and croaks! There's no way to predict it. *(Beat.)* Except possibly with pigeons. Did you know that the passenger pigeon is extinct? The last one died in the Cincinnati Zoo in 1914. At the start of the First World War – in other words, just as mankind took its first concerted step towards it own annihilation. "Passenger." What does that mean? In other words, who's driving? And where are they going? These are the questions I've asked myself over and over again. Did the passenger pigeon just hop off when it saw where the bus was heading? *(Beat.)* Since Noah's ark, pigeons have carried the message of peace. Yes, that was a pigeon. Everybody calls it a dove because they think it sounds better. The names are interchangeable, but people don't like to think of those ugly, lice-infested creatures that live under the elevated and shit on their heads as doves. Do you know what the most common wild pigeon in the United States is? The turtle dove. Also called the mourning dove. A love bird, the turtle dove – in mourning for its love. No! In mourning for love, for love itself! *(Beat.)* I know you're here to talk me into coming back, but how can I do that? For three months I've been trying to discover the secret of harmonious vibrations, and I've got nothing to show for it. Nothing! *Nothing! Zilch!* Do you know what my business partners said when I told them I was going away indefinitely? "Sure, Pete. We'll be waiting." Not, "You're out!", but, "Fine, see you when you're ready." And they smiled and shook my hand. Luck dogs my heels, while **Percy** — *(A bird dropping falls on his head. He stops short, and takes off his hat to examine it, then slowly looks up and addresses Andrea.)* **Did you say, "Shit happens?"** *(He turns the hat around, examining the bird dropping as though trying to grasp the reality of it. Finally, he begins to smile, as the idea dawns with enormous impact. His face is transformed with the wonder of a great discovery.)* **That's true, isn't it? It does! Even to me! Shit has been happening all along, and I just didn't notice! Andrea, I think I want to go home!**

Went Down to the Crossroads
by Philip Goulding

Hopkinson — 20s–30s   Serious

Hopkinson is an ex-cop who has left the police force because of stress and danger. Here he explains the incident that drove him to turn in his badge and gun and go into management instead, taking a job with a local transportation company. Hopkinson struggles with two problems as he speaks: the need to justify to Stedman, a journalist, his choice to leave the police force, and his greater need to find relief from the nightmares, the secret fears, and the lingering desire for revenge that he still experiences from years in police work. The monolog offers the actor opportunities to explore guilt, fear, denial, need, and uncertainty as Hopkinson reassures his vis-à-vis as well as himself. It also offers several discoveries that Hopkinson makes as he retells the story. The speech begins with a strong narrative section, then allows the actor to develop more personal and reflective moments as it moves toward a conclusion that can be either uplifting or foreboding.

HOPKINSON: Then all of a sudden he emerged. Started to come towards me. He had his hands on his head. It was like something out of a film. I mean ... I couldn't think what I was supposed to say for a minute ... He was looking directly at me now. He could see me. He was heading towards me. He ... *(Suddenly shouts:)* "Stop! Hands in the air! Armed Police!" *(Calmly:)* Stupid really, I mean, well ... it was obvious. Anyway, he kept coming. I didn't want that. *(Suddenly shouts:)* "Halt! Stay where you are!" *(Calmly:)* It would have been so easy. Revenge ... I mean, I didn't know

Francis that well, but ... when you've had someone's last thoughts sprayed across your shoulder you feel ... I dunno ... "bonded?" But revenge ... it's like another kind of madness, isn't it? When you stop "stopping to think" and just act ... Just become ... a reflex. I thought about it too long. My finger twitched. I was looking straight at him. Intense. Like I could lose myself. Straight between his eyes. I fired. *(Pause.)* It ... it was a warning shot, of course. Just a warning shot. He crapped it. Stopped in his tracks. I went forward. Funny ... I couldn't believe what he looked like. He was so small. I was expecting Schwarzenegger. Instead he was just ... just nothing. Some kid. Some stupid kid. *(Pause.)* The service, they said I "did a good job." "Thoroughly professional." To deal with that. That wasn't my job. I didn't join the force to be shot at by lunatics. I was out of there. I want to live. I'm not a coward, Ms. Stedman. But I'm a human being. I want to be safe. It's a good feeling. So now I work for the bus company. Assess the feasibility of certain urban and rural routes. Sometimes cuts need to be made. It's still an "us and them" situation. But now when people are disgruntled they write letters to the local newspaper or shout at me at public meetings. I'm still an unpopular bastard. But it's less hazardous. I still have nightmares. Sometimes I'm too scared to sleep. I use the time. I've been learning to paint. I work from photographs. Rural landscapes.

I Saw a Woman Murdered the Other Day
by William Borden

Man — Indeterminate age   Serious

This piece has a wonderfully authentic character to it — it could be a true story. Because of that it allows the actor to use himself fully as the dramatic character, to "actually live the part" and invest himself in the role. In fact, the incident described here could have occurred to any of us. The actor must be careful, though, to keep the piece active and dynamic. The Man is not "musing" over the past but struggling with the dilemma of his own inaction. He's also struggling with the deeper question that he poses at the end: Are any of us prepared to live "in the real world"?

MAN: I saw a woman murdered the other day. Coming out of her apartment building. She was about my age. She had red hair. She was wearing a black dress and dark glasses. She was putting her keys in her purse. She didn't look worried. Maybe she was thinking, I'll go to the grocery, then I'll pick up some lunch. Her purse was still open, and this guy climbed out of his car, and he yelled at her, "Bitch! I saw who you was with last night!" – something like that, and he pulled out a pistol, and she didn't even look surprised, or maybe she didn't see the gun, or she didn't believe it – and he shot her, three, maybe four, times. She fell down the steps. The stuff in her purse spilled all over. He looked at her a few seconds, then he got in the car and drove off. Blood was spreading out in a pool beneath her body. Some teenage boys ran over. I thought they were going to help her, but they grabbed her purse and ran off.

I couldn't have helped her. There was too much blood. I walked away. When I looked back, she was still lying there, her arm at an odd angle, blood pooling around her body, all alone.

I don't think he'll kill again. He killed the woman he loved. Who else is he going to kill?

Maybe I should have gone to the police, but I was afraid. You read these novels, innocent guy at the scene of the crime, the cops pin it on him because they can't find the real murderer, he goes to the chair. I was afraid to go back.

I know, that's a novel, not the real world.

There's not that much difference.

I don't know what I'd do in the real world.

Monologs for Women

"Blind Date"
by Ann Roth
from The Blueberry Café by Women At Play

Alissa — Teens   Serious

Alissa is in a rage, confronting her mother. This monolog gives the actor a strong vis-à-vis as the character opposes her mother and desperately tries to persuade her to get rid of the blind date who has arrived. It also contains clear indications of what Alissa's mother is saying to her, so Alissa's statements take the form of purposeful, focused responses. The speech needs to be structured, however, by the actor in order to avoid presenting an uninteresting "gush" of whining complaint and stubbornness. The actor should try instead to plot out Alissa's development so the monolog eventually leads to the final section, where humor, relief, and incredibility result from the mother-daughter confrontation.

ALISSA: I'm not going back down those stairs, Mom. I'm not. I won't, I can't. Don't make me, please, please, please. Because he's horrible, ugly, horrible, disgusting, that's why. Well, of course his mother didn't tell you that! He has on a bow tie. Oh, God, and white shoes. A bow tie and white shoes. Never, never, never, I'm not budging from this room! (Pause.) Yes, I just left him there. I don't know, I guess he's talking to him ... well, I'm not worried about what Daddy will say. ... What do you mean, how could I do it? I opened the door, took one long look and said excuse me, I've got to get something. Ran upstairs and here I stay. You have to go downstairs and get rid of him, yes you do. No, no, no, I will not budge, stop it, you're not strong enough to drag me.

Stop it, that hurts! Now go, will you ... ? You're laughing. Oh my God, how can you laugh? What? You think Dad is telling those boring football stories to him? The galloping ghost and the flying tackles with no padding.

(Starting to giggle, despite herself:) **How could he? That nerd wouldn't know a football from a hockey puck.** *(Laughing:)* **Now stop it, Mom, this is not funny.** *(Trying to control herself and getting more agitated:)* **Stop laughing, will you, and go downstairs, please. I don't know, tell him anything. Tell him I was stricken, yes stricken, very ill. I am stricken, Mom. My stomach turned over when I opened the front door. What do you mean I can't do this? I'm doing it. I don't care if it's only one evening. No, I will not meet someone else when I'm with him! No one would even consider me if they see me with that creature. Can't you understand that? What? What are you giggling about? Stop that. This is terrible for me and you're laughing. Yes, he does really have on white shoes and a bow tie.** *(Starts giggling again despite herself:)* **Who's Harry Franklin? He what? He wore bow ties and white shoes? You were crazy about him?** *(Trying to stop laughing:)* **That was a hundred years ago, Mom. Now stop it. What do you mean, poor Dad? I'm sure he's doing just dandy. What does he care — it's not his blind date. If you're so worried get down there and tell him I'm sick. Please, you can do it, Mom.** *(Very agitated:)* **I'm not going! Please, please, please. No, I don't care how embarrassing it is. So you play bridge with his mother. So what? What about me?** *Now do it.* **You won't hurt his feelings. Just lie and say goodbye. For me, Mom. Oh God, please, please. I won't move from this spot, I can promise you that. You can't make me. Just go, go, go!** *(She has covered her face and is sobbing. She peers out from behind her hands and sees her mom leaving the room.)* **Oh, thank the lord. Go, go, hurry, yes, yes, yes. She's down there. I can hear her little voice. Now close the door. Do it.**

Yes. Done. *(Pause. Sees Mom.)* **He's really gone? See, you did it. Thank God! Oh, no, Mom, I didn't mean that ... right ... right. God wouldn't lie, but he also wouldn't have fixed me up with that geek. OK?** *(Sheepishly:)* **Did he believe you? Oh no, you gave him what? The left over meat loaf and a box of candy?** *(Starts to giggle through tears, then laughter.)* **The left over meat loaf and a box of candy! The left over meat loaf and a box of candy! Mom, Mom, stop it. You're making me laugh, now stop it ... it's not funny ... No, it isn't.** *(She continues laughing.)*

Fair(l)y (S)tale
by Amanda Kellock

Sleeping Beauty — Indeterminate age   Comic

In this updated version of the familiar tale, the playwright considers the heroine in a modern light in order to examine the ethical choices and "gender politics" that underlie the traditional story. This is the play's opening monolog in which Sleeping Beauty is being interrogated about the "strange circumstances" surrounding her husband's decision to have her committed. The actress can find strong obstacles to play here as she responds to the offstage vis-à-vis who is questioning her.

(A bright spotlight snaps on to reveal SLEEPING BEAUTY at center. She tries to see into the harsh light, responding to an unheard voice as though she is being interrogated.)

SLEEPING BEAUTY: I told you, I got them from a witch. *(Pause.)* Take your pick — there are enough around. *(BEAUTY reacts as though she has been slapped.)* She lives in a little cottage in the woods. *(Pause.)* Yes, the one they say eats little children. *(Pause.)* I don't know, it didn't bother me. *(Pause.)* No, I don't have any of my own. *(Pause.)* What do you mean "why not"? I just don't. It never occurred to me. That's not a crime is it? *(Pause.)* You can't be serious, I mean if I choose — What? *(Pause.)* They were just to help me sleep. That's all. I was having trouble sleeping, so I went to her for help — *(Pause.)* I told you. I was having trouble sleeping. *(Pause.)* Yes, I am aware of the irony, thank you. *(Pause.)* I don't know why. *(Pause.)* I said I don't know — *(Pause.)* I guess I just felt I had slept enough. It was time to be awake. I had reached my sleep quota. So for that, among other things, bedtime was a difficult time. A time I avoided. So, I guess I couldn't sleep because I didn't want to. *(Pause.)* Why the pills, then? Well, I am only human. Can't stay awake forever. And besides, I was very, very tired. *(Pause.)* Was that how many I took? Well, like I said. I was very, very tired.

Fair(l)y (S)tale
by Amanda Kellock

Snow White — Indeterminate age   Comic

In this updated version of the familiar tale, the playwright considers the heroine in a modern light in order to examine the ethical choices and "gender politics" that underlie the traditional story. This is one of the play's opening monologs in which Snow White is being interrogated about the "strange circumstances" surrounding her husband's decision to have her committed. The actress can find strong obstacles to play here as she tries to justify her "strange" behavior to the Off-stage listener, who should be located in the house.

(*A bright spotlight snaps on to reveal SNOW WHITE in a tight spotlight, reminiscing.*)

SNOW WHITE: Somehow it just eased my soul to clean the house – to stand afterwards in a place where orderly people seemed to live. To take something that was worn and unkempt – and make it shine. Like new, as though you could be reborn there. I never really thought it would get me anywhere. But first it got me into trouble – no one likes a nice, quiet, pretty girl I guess! And then it saved me. Those seven little men certainly did appreciate my work. Funny that seven little ones could be so much more appreciative than one big one. But that was different, I suppose. He was a prince after all. And it's not that he didn't like it when I tidied up – he just didn't want me to change anything.

In the Laundromat
by William Borden

Woman — 20s or 30s   Comic

This suspenseful piece will keep the auditors guessing whether you're "playing a character" or "playing yourself." It's a wonderful audition piece because it elicits such honesty from the listener, all the while enabling any actress to invest the character with her own personality. Is the actress a serial killer? Or merely talking about one? If the latter, then it's a remarkably penetrating monolog that relies on strong characterization. If the former ... well? The Woman performs the monolog dressed in a trench coat.

WOMAN: You're sitting in a Laundromat. You're minding your own business. Maybe you're reading a magazine. Maybe you're reading a year-old issue of *Time* magazine. Maybe a woman walks in. A woman in a raincoat with a fistful of hundred-dollar bills. A woman with a preposterous story, about being a stock car driver, a secret agent, a hit woman. Maybe you actually believe this woman. Maybe this woman takes all her clothes off, to wash them. And all the time the washer is going *swish swish* and the dryer is going *thump thump* you can't stop thinking, *she's naked under that raincoat,* and maybe you cop a glimpse of thigh or breast from time to time, you don't think she notices, but she notices, maybe she let the raincoat fall open on purpose, maybe everything she does and says is on purpose, it's as if, well, it's as if it was all written out, as if in a novel, or in a short story, maybe it doesn't last long enough for a novel, maybe it's a short story, and you're thinking, I'm getting some good material here for a novel, or at least a short story — I'd have to marry her to get a novel, but at least I'm getting a short story, I'm getting a peek at the quirky, tough, unpredictable essence of ... a hit woman, maybe she *is* a hit woman — maybe she's really dangerous — maybe you're getting more material than you counted on. Maybe you're getting something no one else has written about. Something different. Something that might make a best seller. But you're afraid. You're afraid you're getting more than you can handle. And yet — suddenly you realize — that you don't know how the story will end. Will you simply walk out of her life — one of those inconclusive endings that leave you hanging, the kind they print in *The New Yorker*? Or will she pull a pistol from that raincoat and drill you right through the heart — something for an anthology of hard-boiled detective stories, a post-modern O. Henry ending? Or will she — maybe — open her raincoat? Will they fall to the grungy floor of the run-down Laundromat in the two-bit, one-horse town and make mad crazy love thrashing atop the year-old *Time* magazines? Or will he have to marry her? Because he knows, and she knows, that if he marries her, and if he loves her, too, of course — loves her insanely, with every breath and every thought and every sentence he writes — he will write one hell of a novel. *(She starts to open her raincoat.)*

Red Frogs
by Ruth Margraff

1   Mabie — Indeterminate age   Comic

    This poetic monolog challenges the actor to focus on sound and image rather than on strict literal sense. The author explains that "the meaning of language is less interesting than its phonetic shape and its sound." And she has described this particular "Marxian" speech of Mabie as "blasphemous" because Mabie is "placing a theory on a working class that can't quite grasp it is problematic." Thus, Ruth Margraff suggests here that older political terminology such as "means of production" or "the people" or "counter-revolutionary terror" might be largely unworkable today — a "dinosaur machine" — and we probably need something new for the age of cyberpunkdom. In this scene from this "burlesque" experimental play, Mabie is desperately trying to convince Penny to forsake her allegiance to Beatifica before she is lost and Beatifica dominates and destroys her.

MABIE: We would need pure action from you, Penny, not this sort of lifeless support. We can tell you see Beatifica's dialect now for what it is, in retrospect of course. Transfusing with your comprehension of practical materials. We knew she'd gotten so surplussive from the superstructure that we leant to you and frankly, when you noticed crucial shifts in point of view from 1st person plural to 3rd person plural "people" that was my voice speaking to you through the torso's pamphlets and I take a singular verb as a collective pronoun. How is the dream elite, you ask? We ask our cell of selves. How is the science or psychology *(She spits.)* of it not elite? Are we not entitled to our opiates of guns and roses? We think as we are stroking at our cell selves and each other calling it mutual use. Calling it demand. Calling it exchange. Calling it movement. The pulp doled out to us by the very last means of production is a dinosaur machine the torso had anointed for us to screw and bolt. The Torso Marxists from the stone age of their industry once offered muscle when there was steel and a railroad to be built. Meanwhile you go off to cyberpunkdom and from there publish secondary sources in 2nd person You You You your paltry points of view pointing the finger to mobilize me now for what? Another backfired, shortsighted error that did not predict counter-revolutionary terror? When is there *not* counter-revolutionary terror? When is there not the side effect of massacre to invert the order? We wield the torso as a tool itself. We don't exactly quote him like he's got some deified solidarity on our indigenous catastrophes. He was a Eurocentric bastard pawn of a dagger. Now our tools are of the mind and for the production of the mind as the omnipotent machine.

Women Behind the Walls
by Claire Braz-Valentine

Valdetta — 20–30   Serious

This monolog is taken from a play that was written from improvisation and storytelling with the women inmates of one of California's state prisons, and much of what is recounted here is a true-to-life incident. The playwright explains that her drama is designed "to make us listen, make us think of the women who are just like us except they made a mistake and now will pay forever." The setting takes place in women's cells. This monolog presents strong challenges for the actor to "live the moment again" and struggle with her own self-doubts and the terrible physical circumstances of the fire as she recalls the incident that landed her in prison. In the original version Valdetta is either of African-American or mixed race descent.

VALDETTA: It was late, around 10 p.m. We had a long day and he was tired. He was sound asleep. I had to go to the store to get some things for breakfast. I didn't want to wake him. It was just a block away and it was freezing out. I threw on my coat and ran down the three flights of stairs and down the street. When I got to the store I grabbed some milk and cereal and fruit, and there was a lady there in front of me, arguing with the clerk. I got nervous. I almost put the groceries down and ran home. *(VALDETTA sobs.)* Oh God, how I wish I had. But I waited another few minutes, and paid the clerk and raced out. I was half way up the block when I remembered the candle. Our building is old and some of the lights don't work. I remember covering him ... I remember seeing his face, his beautiful face, sleeping, seeing his face in the candlelight. *(Terror at the memory:)* The candle ... I had left the candle. It suddenly was as if I was in a dream. I was running but couldn't move fast enough. I reached the apartment and started climbing the stairs and then I smelled the smoke. The awful smell. *(Frantic:)* I remember screaming his name. David, David, over and over, knowing I shouldn't have left him alone, and the stairs going on forever, and then the key, the key getting stuck in the rusty old lock and the smoke coming out. I remember the flames on the wall ... the drapes ... and I ran to him, screaming, "Oh God, please save my son, my baby."

(She is sobbing uncontrollably.) But I saved him. I saved my baby. And everything was going to be fine. Everything was going to be all right. But the Fire Department called Children's Services and they took him. They took my baby. And they put me in here.

Scenes for Men

The Minotaur
by Neil Duffield

1 Theseus — Teens
2 Daedalus — Teens
3
4　　*In this dramatization of the ancient Greek myth, Daedalus*
5 *is the gifted artistic son of King Aegeus of Athens. In this*
6 *moving scene, Daedalus is a grown man and meets his half-*
7 *brother Theseus for the first time. Their initial encounter is*
8 *filled with camaraderie, disbelief, surprise, joy, and even*
9 *suspicion and fear. The scene offers numerous reversals and*
10 *discoveries, as well as a rich subtext for the actors.*
11
12　　*(DAEDALUS is working on the model of a seagull. THESEUS*
13　　*enters.)*
14 THESEUS: *(Looking at the model)* **That's good. It's very good.**
15 DAEDALUS: Thank you.
16 THESEUS: It almost looks alive.
17 DAEDALUS: They go where they please. Over white-capped
18　　waves and mountains. Gliding like kites on the wind.
19　　They're my dream.
20 THESEUS: You dream of being a seagull?
21 DAEDALUS: I dream of having their wings. I dream of soaring
22　　high above the clouds and over the ocean. Up there you
23　　can see beyond the furthest horizon.
24 THESEUS: What do you see?
25 DAEDALUS: Far in the distance I glimpse a gleaming kingdom.
26　　A land of dreams. A land of the sun.
27 THESEUS: What's it like, this land?
28 DAEDALUS: It's the most beautiful place on earth. I can see
29　　palaces and temples. Columns of marble and walls of ashlar.

Throne rooms, shrines, schools, libraries, theatres. Statues of Apollo. Painted frescoes — dolphins, lions, bulls — colours of gold and azure. And everywhere there is light. Light and music — as dazzling as the sky. I glimpse a world of joy, a world of sunlight ... *(Disturbed:)* But then ...

THESEUS: Then what?

DAEDALUS: Then I want to see more. I want to fly higher. I want to glimpse more of that world.

THESEUS: And do you?

DAEDALUS: I fly higher. And higher still. The higher I fly the more I can see. I see children playing in the fields. I hear music — cool and vibrant. I want to fly higher, I want to see even more. But then something starts to happen. Something awful. Something terrifying ...

THESEUS: What? What is it?

DAEDALUS: Something too horrible to speak of. Something so dreadful the very thought of it sets me shivering with terror. *(He stops, unable to continue.)*

THESEUS: And then you wake. You wake up cold — your body wet with sweat. Your heart pounding like a drum. You peer into the darkness, gasping and shaking. You can't accept that the terror wasn't real. You can't believe it was only a nightmare.

DAEDALUS: You know.

THESEUS: My dream is of a monster — it has the body of a man and the head and horns of a bull. It lives below the earth in a black maze of tunnels that has neither beginning nor end. I wander through those corridors filled with fear. I hear the monster bellowing in the dark. I sense its presence. Its stench fills my nostrils. Its foul breath surrounds me in the shadows. I start to run but my feet slip on the damp slime of the floor. The faster I run the more I slither and slide. I hear it pounding and roaring behind me. Fear wells up from my stomach. It fills my ears, my nose, my mouth. I try to scream but my voice is frozen. I slip, I stagger, I fall. I see its horns rising up above me, I feel the hot steam of its breath ...

DAEDALUS: And then you wake.

THESEUS: Then I wake. *(Pause.)*

DAEDALUS: What's your name?

THESEUS: Theseus. ... And yours?

DAEDALUS: Daedalus.

THESEUS: *(Surprised)* A boy? I took you for a girl.

DAEDALUS: You sound like my father. He's always wanted me to be a warrior, the same as him.

THESEUS: My father's a warrior.

DAEDALUS: What's his name?

THESEUS: Aegeus. King of Athens.

DAEDALUS: *(Astonished)* Aegeus?!

THESEUS: That's why I'm here. I've come to meet him. He's never seen me before. I'm not even sure he knows I exist.

DAEDALUS: I'm absolutely certain he doesn't.

THESEUS: What do you mean?

DAEDALUS: King Aegeus is my father too.

THESEUS: What?

DAEDALUS: You and I are brothers.

THESEUS: No, it can't be. It's not true.

DAEDALUS: We have the same father. ... We're brothers!

(DAEDALUS is delighted. THESEUS is completely thrown.)

THESEUS: Then who's your mother?

DAEDALUS: Queen Medea.

THESEUS: Never in my wildest dreams did I imagine I had a brother! He's married? He has a wife?

DAEDALUS: I'll take you to meet them. We'll go straight away. Father won't be able to believe it! *(He tries to go. THESEUS holds back.)* Come. We'll go together.

THESEUS: No. ... Not now. ...

DAEDALUS: What's the matter? You came here to meet him. ... You're his son.

THESEUS: You must never tell him that.

DAEDALUS: How can I not?
THESEUS: Promise me. You must never to tell my father what I've told you.
DAEDALUS: But you're my brother!
THESEUS: Promise me!
DAEDALUS: He needs to know!
THESEUS: Promise!! *(Pause. DAEDALUS sees that THESEUS is in deadly earnest.)*
DAEDALUS: If that's what you wish then I shall say nothing ... What will you do?
THESEUS: I need to think. I need time to think. *(THESEUS turns to go.)*
DAEDALUS: Will I see you again? *(They gaze at each other for a moment. THESEUS exits.)*

The Minotaur
by Neil Duffield

Daedalus — Teens
Apollo — Indeterminate age

In this dramatization of the ancient Greek myth, Daedalus is the gifted artistic son of King Aegeus of Athens. In this scene, Daedalus has come under suspicion by King Minos, who commissioned him to build his labyrinth, where the hideous mythical monster, the minotaur, is confined. Daedalus longs to escape, and in his tower prison he receives the god Apollo who has come to visit and inspire him to invent a pair of wings for his escape.

DAEDALUS: Was Minos right? Did I betray the trust he placed in me?
APOLLO: Only you can know that.
DAEDALUS: How do you choose between a promise made to a king and the life of your own brother?
APOLLO: Choosing which path to follow is never simple — even for a maze builder.
DAEDALUS: But there are right paths and wrong paths — even in a maze.
APOLLO: Right for whom ... ? For Minos? For Theseus? For your father ... ? What is right for one can be wrong for the other.
DAEDALUS: I tried to do what I thought was right for all of them.
APOLLO: Then maybe you should try to do what you think is right for yourself.
DAEDALUS: I'm shut up in a prison. I'm locked at the top of the highest tower in all Crete!

APOLLO: Then escape.

DAEDALUS: Oh fine. Why didn't I think of it ... ? Jump out of the window shall I? Soar like a seagull over the rooftops?

APOLLO: Why not?

DAEDALUS: Perhaps you haven't noticed — I don't happen to have wings.

APOLLO: Then invent them.

DAEDALUS: ... Invent them?

APOLLO: You invented them for ships. *(APOLLO picks up the model of the seagull from its place on the set.)* Who knows more than you how a bird flies? You've studied their movement, their anatomy, the pattern of their flight. You know everything about them.

DAEDALUS: ... I've no tools, no materials. *(APOLLO picks up a couple of feathers.)*

APOLLO: Seagulls perch on your window ledge. They nest on your roof. Their feathers are all around.

DAEDALUS: *(Taking the feathers)* How would I fasten them together? What would hold them to my arms?

APOLLO: What lights your room at night?

DAEDALUS: ... Candle wax ... I could fix them with candle wax!

APOLLO: Then spread your wings and fly high over the rooftops. Above the clouds and over the ocean.

DAEDALUS: Towards the far-distant horizon.

APOLLO: The land of the sun.

DAEDALUS: I'll do it. I'll make wings. I'll escape. I'll fly away from this prison. I'll fly to the land of the sun!

The Trees They Grow So High
by Tony Powell

1 Boy — Teens
2 Stevie — Teens
3
4 The time is 1914, the scene is Wales, and Boy has just enlisted
5 in the British army to fight the Germans in France. Boy cannot
6 read or write, but he feels that "the great adventure" will offer
7 him some life experience greater than anything he could find at
8 home. Young actors will find strong goals to play here — and
9 strong obstacles — as Boy tries to convince his friend Stevie that
10 enlistment is a very good choice. The stakes are huge, and the
11 actors can add rich subtext to the scene by discovering self-doubt
12 in each of their characters: Do Boy and Stevie really believe all
13 that they're saying to each other as they argue? Do they really
14 need each other? Stevie is chopping wood as the scene opens.
15
16 BOY: So what about it, Stevie? Join up with me? Six weeks
17   training, then to France. Come on, Stevie, it's going to be the
18   break we've always wanted. Away from this dead-end hole.
19   Think of it! Traveling, all those girls, uniforms, smart boots,
20   money in your pocket, and away from here. And adventure.
21 STEVIE: What about your mum?
22 BOY: She's too old to join up.
23 STEVIE: Have you told her?
24 BOY: No, not yet, nor Annie. I've only told you.
25 STEVIE: You scared of them?
26 BOY: A little. ...
27 STEVIE: You've signed up to fight a war and you're too scared to
28   tell your mum and your girl!
29 BOY: Well, you know, what they're like. ...
30 STEVIE: Yeah! And do you know what war is like?

1 BOY: It must be better than this. Come on, Stevie, now's our
2 chance to do something useful.
3 STEVIE: Useful! This is useful: cutting wood, mending gates,
4 fixing walls, bringing in the harvest. This is useful – not
5 bloody killing people. You always were the bloody village
6 idiot and now you've proved it. Idiot! Don't you understand
7 anything? *(He returns to chopping wood.)*
8 BOY: When I come back a hero then we'll see who's the idiot.
9 STEVIE: That's the first thing you don't understand, that all
10 heroes are idiots. And as for coming back. ...
11 BOY: Come on, Stevie, it'll be an adventure.
12 STEVIE: I've had adventures with you before. Remember?
13 BOY: We were only little kids then, this is grown-up.
14 STEVIE: If this war is what grown-ups do, I'd prefer to remain a
15 kid. And how many people are you going to desert like you
16 deserted me? They shoot you in the army for that.
17 BOY: I didn't desert you. ...
18 STEVIE: And as you can't read, do you know what you signed?
19 BOY: It was a bit of paper.
20 STEVIE: A bit of paper! And how did you sign it?
21 BOY: *(Embarrassed)* I made my mark with a cross.
22 STEVIE: And that's how it will end – with a wooden one. *(With*
23 *two pieces of wood he makes a cross and thrusts it into BOY's*
24 *arms.)* Bloody idiot! You should be sent to a loony bin.
25 BOY: Shut up! Oh yes, you can read and write but where has it
26 got you? All day cutting wood to be burnt, making gates that
27 lead nowhere. Well, this is my chance to do something, to
28 prove myself.
29 STEVIE: To prove what? To whom?
30 BOY: To all them that call me the idiot boy.
31 STEVIE: *(Calmer and kindlier)* Who's going to look after you? Stop
32 them laughing at you?
33 BOY: I don't need anyone to look after me. But you do. The truth
34 is, that you're afraid, and you have always been.
35 STEVIE: I'm not afraid. ... I'm not. ... See you around. ... I hope.

The Trees They Grow So High
by Tony Powell

1 Boy — Teens
2 Stevie — Teens
3
4   *As in the previous scene, the time is again 1914, but the*
5 *scene is now France, where Boy and Stevie await the battle to*
6 *come. Boy thought he had come to terms with the memory of*
7 *his dead father, but a young French girl he recently met near*
8 *the camp suddenly reminded him of his dad. The theme of the*
9 *"Wood of the Dead" has run through the play, and Boy is*
10 *wondering whether now it foreshadows something about to*
11 *happen. The major acting challenge is to avoid allowing the*
12 *energy to dissipate during the long monolog. The actors must*
13 *sustain the tension by using the past not as a form of nostalgic*
14 *escape but instead as an obstacle against which to struggle,*
15 *and eventually to overcome.*
16
17 **STEVIE: So it's tomorrow then ... ?** *(Silence.)* **What are you**
18   **thinking?**
19 **BOY: I was thinking about that French girl today.**
20 **STEVIE: What about her?**
21 **BOY: She wanted me to have it with her.**
22 **STEVIE: You lucky bugger!**
23 **BOY: I didn't.**
24 **STEVIE: Bloody hell! I said you were insane, now you've**
25   **proved it. Why not?**
26 **BOY: She struck a match.**
27 **STEVIE: Was she a French fire-eater then?**
28 **BOY: I suddenly saw my dad.** *(STEVIE looks totally bemused.)*
29   **You see, I don't remember him as a whole person. I just**

remember him in little flares of light, as his face lit up every time he struck a match for his pipe. And she struck a match and for an instant I saw my dad standing there. And Mum kept saying how proud he would have been, and I wanted to have her but ... I keep seeing him. ... Sorry, that must seem strange.

STEVIE: No. No, it's not strange. I ... I ... keep thinking about my little sister Frances. Don't know why. I remember how no one would tell me what had happened to her. They kept saying she had gone away. And I kept asking, "Where?" And they kept saying, "Just away." And the next day all the adults kept going into the parlour and then they would come out crying. So very early the next morning I crept into the parlour. The curtains were drawn, but through the join came this most piercing shaft of light. And it shone on the table. The best one. The Sunday Tea and Christmas Dinner table. And on the table was a beautiful box, oak carved and polished. I thought that they had got me a present, because she had gone away, but I couldn't reach it. So I got Grandma's stool and stood on it, and looked in the box. And there with her hair all spread out on a pillow was my sister. I told her off, because they had all said she had gone away, but she was hiding in that box. And she wouldn't answer, so I ran upstairs and woke up Mum and Dad and shouted at them that I had found Frances and that she hadn't gone away, that she was hiding in the box. And I remember Mum screaming hysterically and Dad trying to calm her and calling me names ... and. ...

BOY: You've never told me any of this before.

STEVIE: I've never really remembered it before. Why now?

BOY: In all the stories the ghosts always appear on the night before battle.

STEVIE: The battle before the trees move. ... *(Pause.)*

BOY: Did I tell you that I met old Smokey Smithy before we left?

He talked about remembering us as kids at school and how upset it made him to see us march away, and at the time I just wished he'd shut up because I was going to march away. But now I wish I had thanked him. You would never have thought that the people that you spend all those years mocking can suddenly seem very important. *(The rain gets louder.)* Hark at it! I wonder if it's raining at home? I bet Mum is sitting by the smoky fire, furiously knitting. When she knits she's constantly looking at the clock. She knits her life away, and every second is caught in the stitches. This balaclava contains all those seconds during the night before we came away. When I wear it now I put that whole night around my head. *(He buries his face in the balaclava. He looks up and more memories come back. STEVIE takes the balaclava and puts it to his face.)* When I met Annie, we went up the hill and we tried to count the trees. We talked about when we were children and about growing up, and about marriage. Then she said we were too young. She was right, and when we return she will still be too young, but after this I will be too old. I wonder if it is raining at home? Shimmering on the slate roofs and hissing as it hits the thatch. Pouring on the cobbles and gushing down to the stream. And little splashes down the chimney, and the smoke from the fires swirling across the fields. ... We couldn't count all the trees. That is the most terrible thing about this place ... what the French girl said ... all the trees have gone. Whole forests and orchards splintered into matchwood. A million matchsticks. ... I can see my dad again. Mum said he would be proud, but he just looks so sad. Where we're being sent in the morning ... there's something I haven't told you. The girl told me what that place means. Le Bois Mort ... in English it means "The Wood of the Dead." Stevie, we've come back to Dead Man's Wood and this time I really do see my dad, and I'm scared again, like I was that night.

STEVIE: The night you deserted me. Everyone knows what it did to you – it stopped you reading and writing, but no one understands what it did to me. ... On that day you signed up. The last thing you said to me was that I wouldn't join because I was scared, and I just walked away from you. You see, it was true. I was scared. So I enlisted to prove that I'm not. But I am. I knew no fear when I saw my sister's body, but that night in the woods you taught me to be frightened of death.

BOY: I didn't teach you anything ... the trees did. As a joke you told me that my dad was in that wood still calling for me. You lied to me. I understand now why you did it. Because they lied to you about your sister, you had to lie to me about my dad. It was what you thought grown-ups did when faced with death. And it's true, they do. No one at home knows the truth about this war. But your lie went wrong because it scared you, as their lie will go wrong and scare them when they realize what this is really about.

STEVIE: I am so scared, like that night ... you left me.

BOY: I didn't leave you. *(Pause.)* Don't you understand? The trees took you. They took you to teach you the fear of death. The trees are far older than us and they know everything. When they blow up all the trees, they are not just destroying the landscape, they're destroying the wisdom of the centuries. *(He looks at STEVIE.)* But now we know, and this time in Dead Man's Woods it will be different. This time we'll get out together.

STEVIE: I don't think so. This time we are not children.

BOY: In such a short time we've come a long way since then.

STEVIE: But I don't think that there's much further to go. This is it. This is where it ends; where the fear began ... in the woods.

Surfing, Carmarthen Bay
by Roger Williams

1 Steven — 18
2 Morgan — 18
3
4 *Steven and Morgan have been best friends for years.*
5 *They're graduating soon, and Steven is going off to college*
6 *while Morgan is heading for Australia. Steven has been*
7 *romantically involved for some time with their mutual friend,*
8 *Angela, who worries about him going off to college and*
9 *finding a new girl. The scene is a beach on Carmarthen Bay in*
10 *Wales, where the young people often come to surf and have*
11 *parties. It is night and a graduation party is underway down*
12 *the beach. Angela has just playfully tossed Steven's car keys*
13 *into the sand somewhere and run off to return to the party.*
14
15 **STEVEN:** Mad. Mad as a hatter.
16 **MORGAN:** It's the way she's made.
17 **STEVEN:** Her tongue hasn't stopped wagging all night.
18 **MORGAN:** So you haven't told her yet?
19 **STEVEN:** No, I haven't.
20 **MORGAN:** You chickened out?
21 **STEVEN:** No. I just ... I just thought it was unnecessary. We'll both
22 be going our separate ways soon anyway. We'll drift apart.
23 People always do. *(Pause.)* What do you think of the party?
24 **MORGAN:** It's okay.
25 **STEVEN:** I suppose you'll have to get used to beach parties and
26 barbies.
27 **MORGAN:** Yeah.
28 **STEVEN:** When d'you go?
29 **MORGAN:** End of September.

STEVEN: Wish I had a Dad who'd let me go to Australia. Bloody hell. It's the chance of a lifetime. Bet you can't wait? Are you taking your board?

MORGAN: It's too expensive.

STEVEN: You'll hire one then?

MORGAN: Suppose.

STEVEN: *(Enthusiastically)* There'll be some cracking waves. It'll be brilliant. Australia's like the home of surfing, it'll be one hundred times better than this place. Not many people our age get to travel half way round the world. You're a globetrotter, mun!

MORGAN: When are you off to uni?

STEVEN: October. The fourth, I think. Dad's taking me in the car. If I find the keys, that is. God! Angela does some stupid things!

MORGAN: Looking forward to it?

STEVEN: What? Essays and libraries? I'd rather be in Australia, "mate." Wow. You're so bloody lucky. It'll be odd us lot splitting up, though. Going out alone.

MORGAN: We've been friends a long time, Steve.

STEVEN: Ever since primary school.

MORGAN: Ages isn't it?

STEVEN: It's a weird feeling. Like the end of an era or something.

(Pause. MORGAN walks back. Looks out at the sea.)

MORGAN: It's calm out there tonight.

STEVEN: It's sleeping. *(Pause.)*

MORGAN: That's what Andrew used to say. *(Pause.)*

STEVEN: Wonder what he'd be doing now? He'd probably be on that plane to Australia with you. He loved surfing. He was responsible for getting us into it in the first place.

MORGAN: He was so serious about it. We were only in it for a laugh.

STEVEN: I'll never forget the time he thought we should practice "our balancing technique" and he made us all take turns balancing on your mother's ironing board.

MORGAN: All the top surfers do it.

STEVEN: It was a laugh till your Mum came home early, and you did your load and fell off. *(Pause.)*

MORGAN: It's criminal.

STEVEN: It was an accident, Moggs. Anyone could have been driving around that corner.

MORGAN: They were drunk, Steve.

STEVEN: It was over a year ago. *(Trying to break the tension)* How many hours is the flight? About twenty, isn't it? *(Pause.)* Expect you'll get a film or something to ... watch. *(Silence. There is a sudden burst of laughter offstage, breaking the mood.)*

STEVEN: Looks like Angela's causing trouble.

MORGAN: She knows how to enjoy herself.

STEVEN: That's got to be the understatement of the year. She'll go wild at college. Wilder. Insane. You won't find anyone else like her. Not even in Australia. *(Pause.)* Lucky bastard. I'd do anything to be in your shoes. *(Burst of laughter offstage.)* What's she doing now?

MORGAN: Squirting tomato sauce over Rhodri's chest.

STEVEN: God, she can be so embarrassing when she wants to be.

MORGAN: She's not embarrassing, just. ...

STEVEN: Impulsive?

MORGAN: You could say that, yeah. I'll miss her. *(Pause.)* You know she loves you?

STEVEN: Yeah, yeah.

MORGAN: Steven, she does. Reckon you two are Mr. and Mrs. material. *(Pause.)* You really should tell her.

STEVEN: I will.

MORGAN: When?

STEVEN: When the time is right. I don't want to spoil tonight for her.

MORGAN: Just don't be crap about it.

STEVEN: I won't, okay? *(Pause.)*

MORGAN: I suppose I'll have to pick up the pieces.

1 STEVEN: Don't try and make me feel guilty, Moggs.
2 MORGAN: I'm not.
3 STEVEN: Good.
4 MORGAN: *(Pause)* It's just that. ...
5 STEVEN: What?
6 MORGAN: You've been through a lot together.
7 STEVEN: I was wondering when you'd dredge that up.
8 MORGAN: You can't forget it, Steve. It happened, for Christ sake!
9 STEVEN: I know it happened. You don't have to patronize me.
10 MORGAN: I'm not patronizing you.
11 STEVEN: What are you doing then?
12 MORGAN: I want you to see that you and Ange have gone
13   through hell together, and you just can't expect to throw
14   all of that away!
15 STEVEN: And you'd know all about Angela and me, wouldn't
16   you? This may surprise you, Moggs, but you're not an
17   expert on everything.
18 MORGAN: I don't pretend to know what's going on between
19   Angela and you! Maybe you are finished, but you've got to
20   admit that you did have something good going, there's
21   something special there. She was carrying your baby, Steve.
22 STEVEN: I know what you're doing, Morgan. You're trying to
23   keep Angela and me intact. You want me to pretend that
24   everything's fine so that you and her can make believe
25   that everything's just as it used to be, like nothing's
26   changed. Angela's my first girlfriend, and we shouldn't be
27   tying ourselves down to stupid promises now. It's got to
28   end, Moggs, and it'd be worse to string her along. God!
29   Why am I making excuses? I don't have to explain myself
30   to you. *(Awkward silence.)*
31 MORGAN: We must've covered every inch of this beach. Me.
32   You. Andrew. The Three Musketeers. Straight after school
33   we'd run home, dump our bags and rush over here to meet
34   up – rush to the sea. *(Pause.)* It was like a second home. It
35   was us and the beach, just us, no Mums, Dads. No worries.

(Pause.) It was like we could do anything on the beach, like there were no rules. Remember when Andrew had that obsession with the A-Team, and he used to make us pretend to be them? He was Hannibal, I was Face, and you were either Howling Mad Murdoch, or B.A., depending what mood you were in. It was simple then. But that's all changed, hasn't it? We grew up. You met Angela, and Angela and you met sex. *(Pause.)* I don't want to stir up trouble, but ... but when Angela lost the baby, you stood by her. You were so good with her. If it wasn't for you, I don't think she could have handled it. I was tough for her, Steve. ...

STEVEN: And it wasn't for me? We were sixteen.

MORGAN: Yeah. I know.

STEVEN: So what are you trying to say, Moggs? Spit it out.

MORGAN: I'm just trying to protect her, I suppose. I don't want to see her hurt.

STEVEN: And I do?

MORGAN: No! *(Beat.)* No.

STEVEN: You can't hold on to the past, Moggs. You can't freeze time so that nothing changes. We've grown older. Things have changed between us. We don't run down to the beach and pretend to be crap telly stars any more. That's how things are. We've grown up together, gone through school together, developed chest hair together. *(Pause.)* And now we've passed our exams, we're going our own ways. It's not the end of everything. Life's just starting for us.

Wait Wait Bo Bait
by Lindsay Price

1 Steve — Teens
2 Edgar — Teens

This extract is taken from a play consisting of scenes and monologs about waiting. As the scene begins, Steve and Edgar are high school students seated on chairs outside the principal's office. They both give a big sigh and then begin speaking.

STEVE: How long have they been in there?
EDGAR: Almost half an hour.
STEVE: Half an hour. How long does it take to decide a punishment? Mrs. Dufour always struck me as a rather decisive woman. Two weeks detention – zap! You're suspended – pow!
EDGAR: Your dad is ultra-decisive. He's the king of decisiveness.
STEVE: I know. Can I have the car, Dad? No. Two seconds tops – whammo! What the hell are they talking about?
EDGAR: Maybe they're not talking about you. Maybe they wrapped you up in the first five minutes and now they're talking about vacations. *(STEVE looks at EDGAR.)* It's possible. They could be comparing vacation spots. "I like Hawaii. Jamaica is nice this time of year."
STEVE: You're just in a good mood 'cause they haven't reached your parents and you're not going to get yelled at 'til later.
EDGAR: What's the worst that could happen? You've never been in trouble before. Sure, your first time out has been a bit of a doozy, but really, how hard on you can they be?
STEVE: My dad's going to kill me.
EDGAR: Be serious.

1 STEVE: Seriously, he could kill me.
2 EDGAR: Not gonna happen. Think smaller scale.
3 STEVE: Maybe he'll hide all my shoes ... I don't know.
4 EDGAR: "Son, we've decided your punishment. We're going to
5   hide all your shoes."
6 STEVE: Just because your Dad is all, "Boys will be boys! Hey
7   man, I was young once too. Peace-out!"
8 EDGAR: I don't know, Brillo. I've never set fire to a washroom
9   before. My Dad did a lot when he was young, but I'm
10   pretty sure he never set fire to a washroom.
11 STEVE: But we didn't mean to set fire to a washroom.
12 EDGAR: If only that counted.
13 STEVE: Who knew toilets were so flammable?
14 EDGAR: Hindsight is twenty-twenty.
15 STEVE: What are they doing in there? I wish they'd just come
16   out and get it over with. Just come out right now and get
17   whatever it is, whatever punishment, out in the open. I
18   just want to know. The waiting is killing me!
19 EDGAR: Ah-ha! Chinese water torture! I think there is no
20   punishment. They're just sitting in there, making you
21   sweat it out.
22 STEVE: *(Standing up)* Enough is enough. This is inhuman. If
23   they're going to punish me, fine. Just get it over with. I
24   deserve to know. It's my basic human right to know and I
25   want to know right now!
26 EDGAR: Aw, crap, the door's opening.
27 STEVE: *(Sitting down)* I changed my mind. I can wait.

Another Way Out
by Max Bush

1 Kyle — 18
2 J.T. — 20
3
4 *Kyle has just graduated from high school. J.T., former*
5 *boyfriend of Kyle's sister, is a gang leader. The meeting takes*
6 *place in a park on a weekend afternoon. J.T. has been talking*
7 *to Douglas, a young inventor and science whiz. Fearing for*
8 *Douglas' safety, Kyle is trying to find out why J.T. is interested*
9 *in Douglas. Kat is a fifteen-year-old girl who is trying to enter*
10 *the gang. Kyle has brought a baseball bat to the park.*
11
12 J.T.: So tell me, did Kat come by here?
13 KYLE: I haven't seen her today.
14 J.T.: *(Looking offstage, trying to see her)* **First we lose her**
15   **mother, now her. This park is the Twilight Zone.**
16 KYLE: What's up with Kat? I hear she knows Douglas. Do you
17   know Douglas, J.T.?
18 J.T.: Kat, Kat, where could you be?
19 KYLE: Do you know Douglas?
20 J.T.: *(Indicating bat)* **Schoolboy, playing some ball?**
21 KYLE: Yeah, yeah, I got a game later.
22 J.T.: Got a baseball game later. So you bring your bat early for some
23   batting practice. That's a good looking bat. May I see your
24   bat? *(He holds out his hand, KYLE hesitates, then gives it to*
25   *him.)* **You could punish the ball with this bat. Top weighted,**
26   **excellent balance ... long enough for you, Schoolboy?**
27 KYLE: Sure.
28 J.T.: You say you got a game today?
29 KYLE: Yeah.

1 J.T.: Where's your glove?
2 KYLE: I need to talk to you, J.T. About business. I need to talk
3   to you about some business.
4 J.T: Mysterious Kyle. You are a mystery today. Coming here
5   with your good looking bat and you've no glove, sending
6   Cindy Lou with Tonya, talking business, you never talk
7   business, all these years, you've never talked business.
8 KYLE: You said you —
9 J.T.: Explain that to me.
10 KYLE: You said you—
11 J.T.: Explain that to me. And start your sentence with the word "I."
12 KYLE: I ... need some money for my trip to Europe. I thought
13   maybe, if I could buy something from you, I could sell it to
14   somebody else and make some profit.
15 J.T.: Well, that *is* what we call *business*. But a gentleman in
16   your position would ordinarily find another job, work
17   overtime, paint his grandmother's house, ask his loving
18   parents for money. You are your sister's brother, are you
19   not? Yet, you turn to crime. You want to be a criminal,
20   Kyle? Does that excite you? *(J.T. suddenly throws the bat to*
21   *KYLE in such a way as KYLE has to use both hands above his*
22   *head to catch the bat. J.T. pats down the sides and front of*
23   *KYLE, forcefully turns him around, pats down his back. J.T.*
24   *steps back.)* You working for the police, Kyle?
25 KYLE: No.
26 J.T.: Then what are you doing, Schoolboy?
27 KYLE: What products — other than drugs — do you deal?
28 J.T.: *(Looks at him for a moment, smiles, considers whether or*
29   *not to answer him directly)* You're right. Drugs are mean:
30   the competition, the cops, the time. Drug time with the
31   man is long. Drug time is cruel, you know what I mean? So
32   we offer a multitude of products. Because we are in the
33   profit business. It's all about the money, we get the money,
34   we take care of the money, everybody gets money and
35   stays out of lock up. And if somebody gets taken down,

they're not gone until their bones are old, they're away for the winter. It's about profit from safer products.

KYLE: You have any guns?

J.T.: You're jerking me.

KYLE: Do you have any guns? *(J.T. looks at him, laughs, again considers how to answer KYLE.)*

J.T.: Yeah, we got that. Big guns, little guns, fast guns, crates of guns, you want a gun, Schoolboy? Need a higher grade in your Shakespeare class?

KYLE: What do you carry?

J.T.: I don't pack. No guns, no cell phones, no pilots.

KYLE: What other products?

J.T.: What do you want? Because we offer only what people want. They want DVD players, the flatscreen TV, they want something transported out of town, out of state, out of the country, they want fresh money, they want slots, roulette wheels, they want the girl, we got that, too.

KYLE: Girl?

J.T.: Yeah, our newest specialty, hot selling, lots of business; and not just the old men, either. It's about the love, can't get enough of the love, everybody wants love. A man like you – with limited disposable income – with a girlfriend like that – Cindy Lou I Love You – you don't want any problems. She's pretty, she's smart, she's a woman with a future, she's going to be successful in life, she's a woman you marry, isn't that right? But I can give you something that won't come back on you, something nice, well worth the price. And there'll be no questions, no phone calls, no frantic, spittin' jealousies, you know what I mean?

KYLE: How much?

J.T.: What is it exactly you want with her? I mean, you want something quick, you want to play games, you want two?

KYLE: One. The usual.

J.T.: For you, I trust you, and you're not in the work force yet, so to speak, let's say, because we're just starting here ...

1   something reasonable.
2 KYLE: How old is she?
3 J.T.: Well, yeah, how old do you want her?
4 KYLE: Fifteen.
5 J.T.: Yeah, okay, fifteen, yeah, we got that, but that's a little
6   more expensive because, as you put it, it's not usual.
7 KYLE: *(Truly stunned)* I don't believe this.
8 J.T. All right, I see your point. Maybe this time — because it's
9   part of the initiation, she's sexing in, if you know what I
10   mean, sexing in — you know what that is?
11 KYLE: It's what she has to do to join your gang.
12 J.T.: So it helps us, it helps you, it helps her, you and I get
13   started on a new relationship, you tell your friends, we do
14   more business, yeah, so, we'll keep it reasonable for this
15   time, this first time only, for this unusual arrangement.
16 KYLE: *(To himself, trying to figure out what battle to fight)* What
17   am I supposed to do?
18 J.T.: Say yes and come across with cash. That's all.
19 KYLE: I'll have to think about that. Because I find it difficult to
20   believe. Because I can't believe being in your gang is that
21   important to anybody who's fifteen.
22 J.T.: Believe it, Schoolboy.
23 KYLE: Do you do anything with computers?
24 J.T.: We have a variety of electronic devices; any that you would
25   need, still in the box.
26 KYLE: Do you provide services?
27 J.T.: What services?
28 KYLE: Computer services. Could you do something on the
29   computer for me, like hack into a bank or maybe a business?
30 J.T.: Why don't you tell me exactly what you want?
31 KYLE: Could you hack into something?
32 J.T.: It's whatever you want, Kyle. I answered you, now you tell
33   me, batboy, what is happening with you today?
34 KYLE: I told you, I need to make some money.
35 J.T.: You're lying.

KYLE: Yes, I am.

J.T.: You don't lie to me.

KYLE: Then I'm not telling you anything.

J.T.: What do you want?

KYLE: I don't want to do business with you.

J.T.: All right. *(Short silence.)* But remember, if you're not in my business, you're out of my business. And you stay out of my business.

KYLE: I've never given you any trouble, J.T.

J.T.: Not like your sister. A world of trouble. And no profit with her. All expenses.

KYLE: Yeah, she's gone, and she's not coming back, until you're gone. She knows you; and she knows what you do.

J.T.: I know where she is.

KYLE: Well, that's not true.

J.T.: Hiding from J.T.? I know where she is. But I do not go there. Because ... I ... like her. And, if I go there, I ... will hurt her. Not that way, Schoolboy, I never hit her. But I see, who I am, hurts her.

KYLE: *(Seeing a softer demeanor in J.T.)* Who is Douglas to you?

J.T.: What?

KYLE: You know, that nerd, Douglas, what's he mean to you?

J.T.: Tell your sister ... *(This is difficult for him.)* I miss her. She was ... clean.

KYLE: Does he know something or did he see something? *(J.T. is still lost in thought.)* He's just a strange guy, he wouldn't hurt anybody — he would never mess with you. He doesn't know anything about you and what you do.

J.T.: Like I told you, Kyle, if you're not in my business. ... And whatever is going on with you today, you bring it directly to me.

KYLE: Oh, I don't think there's any way out of doing that, J.T. I'll be bringing it right to you.

Scenes for Women

Looking Through You
by Max Bush

1   Sue Ellen — Teens
2   Kara — Teens
3
4   *This short scene can be played with a rich subtext made up*
5   *from the two characters' shared school experiences. It contains*
6   *numerous references the actors can use to construct character*
7   *biographies. Additionally, it challenges actors to listen and*
8   *react — particularly in the case of Kara — while the actor*
9   *playing Sue Ellen must motivate her words by grounding*
10 *them in friendship and understanding. Why does Sue Ellen*
11 *reveal these observations to Kara? And what motivates Kara to*
12 *listen so patiently and then "run for the mirror" at the end? In*
13 *the play, the scene takes place in the park while the characters*
14 *are waiting for their friends. Sue Ellen and Kara have*
15 *overheard an "in-crowd" girl talking to someone extremely*
16 *emotionally and dramatically.*
17
18 **SUE ELLEN: Don't you think she was talking to her mother?**
19 **KARA: Don't you just want her to be talking to her mother?**
20 **SUE ELLEN: You just want her to be talking to herself the way**
21   **you do.**
22 **KARA: How did you know I talk to myself?**
23 **SUE ELLEN: You do it even when I'm with you.**
24 **KARA: You're not supposed to see me do that.**
25 **SUE ELLEN: That's why I pretend I don't see it.**
26 **KARA: Do you listen?**
27 **SUE ELLEN: Sometimes.**
28 **KARA: What have you heard me say?**
29 **SUE ELLEN: You talk to yourself like you're alone.**

1 KARA: What have you heard me say?
2 SUE ELLEN: I don't want to repeat it. It would creep me out.
3 KARA: You never heard me say anything.
4 SUE ELLEN: You do it into the mirror all the time. You can't walk past a mirror without saying something into it. It's all right, you're weird, Kara, that's all. I won't tell anyone. But everybody knows it anyway. Now what were we talking about? I can't remember.
9 KARA: You've never seen me or heard me say anything.
10 SUE ELLEN: *(She does this without sarcasm, almost reverentially)* "I know you think you look terrible; but I can see you on the inside and you're all right." *(Short silence. KARA gives nothing away.)* "I know you are hurt on the inside, but you look all right on the outside." *(Short silence. KARA still doesn't respond.)* "You can listen to them. You can even learn from them. But you don't have to be afraid of them. I'll be there with you and I know the truth. And I'll always be here for you to talk to. Look into my eyes; you can trust me with your secrets. You see? Look into my eyes. You're not alone."
21 KARA: Yeah ... yeah, you've heard me.
22 SUE ELLEN: It's all right. It doesn't really creep me out. I just don't know if I'm supposed to hear you or not or what.
24 KARA: I guess I thought, since I was talking into the mirror, to myself, I thought I was ... hidden.
26 SUE ELLEN: I tried it in the mirror, but it doesn't make me feel better. Not as much as when you help me, like with my mother. *(KARA begins to walk off.)* Where are you going?
29 KARA: To find a mirror.

Markers
by Shirley King

Paula — Mid-20s
Sandy — Late 20s

Paula and Sandy are sisters. Paula is the more "straight" of the two, being a successful attorney not too long out of law school. Sandy works in a supermarket. The scene is Paula's apartment, shortly following a terrorist attack on the city. As the scene begins, Paula is searching for something: picking up chair cushions, getting down on hands and knees, looking under a small table, standing, muttering to herself.

PAULA: Why? Why is it always me? Why today?

SANDY: *(Entering)* Paula, come on. I'm double parked. You know how quick those meter maids are.

PAULA: And good morning to you. *(Takes in SANDY's appearance.)* Who are we today, Pocahontas? No, I won't even ask. Where's Dad?

SANDY: He wants to stay in touch with Milton. *(She sets a ring loaded with keys on the coffee table.)* How come you're not ready?

PAULA: Don't start, Sandy. Not today. I've looked everywhere. Maybe one rolled under this chair. *(Gets down on hands and knees.)* Who's Milton?

SANDY: Daddy's new special friend on the Internet. Lives in Miami with his sister Frances. *(Pause.)* People were running down the street covered with ashes. The photographer must have been running too, the pictures were so jerky. Terrorists have no respect for human life.

PAULA: No kidding. *(Finds two canisters, holds them up.)* Here they are! *(Puts them in a duffel bag.)*

SANDY: You just always expect the worst. That's so like you, Paula.

PAULA: Absolutely. Terrorists kill innocent people because I don't have a sunny disposition. You're right, I do expect the worst. And yesterday the worst happened. There's a couple of canisters missing. Could you possibly help me look?

SANDY: *(Follows Paula, searching, and finds a canister)* Look! Here's one. *(Holds it up.)* At least I care.

PAULA: And you think I don't just because I'm not falling apart every five minutes? I'm not a weeper, Sandy. You should know this by now.

SANDY: I wonder if Mom would mind about Milton. Dad's been so lonely.

PAULA: Mom's way past minding. *(PAULA takes the canister and puts it in the duffel bag.)* Okay, why do we have to do this? Tell me again. Why today?

SANDY: The markers are in the car and we promised Mom, remember? *(Looks in duffel bag.)* One, two, three. Cleo, Boomer, Angel ... where's Louie? How can we go without Louie? He was Mom's favorite.

PAULA: Louie? I don't remember a Louie.

SANDY: That's because you were in prison then.

PAULA: For a brief time, I visited prisoners in San Quentin. When I was in Criminal Law. Louie must have had a short life. Come on, don't just flutter around – help me look. Why do I always get the depressing stuff to do? Why is it always me?

SANDY: *(Drifts around the room, pulls up the edge of the rug, looks under it)* About Louie, he came from the pound and he was older. And it's not just you doing the so-called depressing stuff. This is an action we can both take. When did you last see Louie?

PAULA: Never. What was he like?

SANDY: Tiny and quivery but always trying so hard to be dignified? He just cracked me up. I think Mom only had

    four in canisters: Boomer, Cleo, Angel and Louie.
PAULA: *(Answering the phone)* Hello? Hi, Dad. No, we're on our way to the cabin. Want to come? Vegas? No, you can't. All flights have been canceled. No Dad, all flights everywhere. Dad, why are you calling? Oh. Well, Sandy's fine. We were just about to leave —
SANDY: *(Cuts her off, grabs phone)* Wait. Let me talk. Hi, Daddy. How's Milton? Well, good. Daddy, was one of Mom's dogs named Louie? Oh, okay. Lester. I thought it was Louie.
PAULA: Lester, Louie — who cares?
SANDY: *(Puts her index finger across her lips in a "hush" signal)* We're planning to put up little markers. Markers. No, Daddy, markers. Daddy, that's okay. I'll tell you all about it tomorrow. Love you lots. Paula loves you too. She just didn't get a chance to say it. Here's a super big hug. *(Hugs herself.)* Bye.
PAULA: Dad's been watching CNN nonstop and he still doesn't believe it.
SANDY: I keep hoping it's all a bad dream. You took the day off?
PAULA: Two days. Nobody could get it together so we just closed down. And Friday will be total hell. I can see people flocking in, wanting their wills updated.
SANDY: I'm off too. Last hired, first to go and don't say "Again?" Baggers and fruit labelers aren't big fish in the labor pool, but it's useful work. Sticking those stickers on for scanning tells the checkers this is a Washington State 4044 peach, and so on.
PAULA: They don't know?
SANDY: FYI, there's cling or freestone, yellow or white, plus hundreds of varieties. So, no, they don't. Not always, and I don't appreciate your sarcasm. I happen to like a simpler job. I'll never be on the Supreme Court like you might be, and that's just fine with me.
PAULA: Maybe we should re-think this. *(Puts one arm around SANDY.)* Doesn't this strike you as crazy, burying dogs' ashes today?

SANDY: We promised Mom. *(SANDY pulls away.)*
PAULA: You promised Mom last March before she died and then dumped those canisters on me like they were live tarantulas.
SANDY: My God, Paula — this is all too much. You know, I could have saved those people.
PAULA: Whoa. Okay, that's it. Tell you what, I'll run down and move your car and you stay here tonight. Give me your keys.
SANDY: But I knew last week. I could see it happening — just the way it did happen.
PAULA: You had a premonition? You *know* that's sheer coincidence.
SANDY: I'm telling you, I dreamed it. *(Drops into a chair.)* Listen to me, please. *(Gets up, goes to PAULA, takes her hands in hers.)* I know this sounds crazy but I could see planes crashing into buildings. Not here in San Francisco. Somewhere else. Why didn't I tell someone?
PAULA: Thank God you didn't.
SANDY: But I might have saved thousands of people.
PAULA: No, Sandy. No, you wouldn't have. Nobody would have believed you and besides the dream wasn't specific. What could they do, ground every single plane because you had a dream?
SANDY: But at least I could've tried.
PAULA: Right. So the FBI could park in your apartment forever — or worse, haul you off to prison?
SANDY: But what if it happens again?
PAULA: No more death dreams. I mean it.
SANDY: Some dreams have minds of their own. Did we find all four dogs? Remember how Mom used to spell things? Like C-o-o-k-i-e and B-y-e B-y-e in the C-a-r? Louie loved going bye-bye.
PAULA: When did you last eat? Maybe you're just hungry. Or dehydrated. Let me go find a diet soda.
SANDY: The way things are going, I'll take a real soda.

PAULA: You'll take diet. That's all I have. Toss me the keys to your Montero.

SANDY: They're on the table. You know, we need to go right now. Otherwise we'll end up having to stay overnight.

PAULA: So? *(PAULA grabs SANDY's keys, tosses them in her purse.)*

SANDY: We can't stay overnight. There's no TV at the cabin.

PAULA: Sandy, seeing it over won't bring back one person killed by those fanatics –

SANDY: Who also killed themselves. At least they had options. You suppose even one terrorist got on a plane thinking, "We don't really have to do this today if we don't want to? Could we maybe just think this through one more time?"

PAULA: You want to know? They saw this as a great career move. Kill thousands of people, get a free pass to Paradise – or wherever the hell terrorists think they go.

SANDY: But they had families, people they loved. And you know, they hated us. Why, Paula? How did they get so bitter? How did you?

PAULA: Gee, I don't have a clue. I mean, some folks might think hating a huge, rich superpower makes sense. Not me. I'm on our side. Look, if burying canisters is on the agenda today I'm willing. But let's go while it's still daylight. We'll stop for tacos on the way. *(She grabs a jacket from the chair.)* You'll need a sweater at the cabin. Did you bring one? Why do I ask – of course, you didn't. Here. *(PAULA puts her jacket around SANDY's shoulders, walks over to a coat tree and takes another jacket for herself.)* And I'm not bitter, just realistic.

SANDY: You're bitter and you're cynical. And you'll just get more bitter and cynical and nothing will ever change for you. You'll die that way.

PAULA: Here's a news flash: I'll die anyway and so will you. Life's a losing proposition. *(Pause.)* Okay, so tell me, do we actually have a plan?

SANDY: First we bury Boomer, Cleo, Angel and Louie with

respect. Did we find Louie?

PAULA: Lester.

SANDY: *(Lifts the duffel bag, looks inside, pulls out a canister, inspects it, holds it up.)* **Look, Louie. It says Louie. I knew I was right! Here it was all the time. Louie, we're taking you to Lake Tahoe.**

PAULA: **If the Bay Bridge is still there.** *(SANDY starts off, carrying the canister and duffel bag. Hands the bag to PAULA who sets it down to button her jacket. SANDY starts to pick up the bag but drops the canister. The lid comes off.)*

SANDY: **Oh, no! Louie.** *(SANDY picks up the empty canister, turns it upside down, then looks inside.)* **Louie?** *(To PAULA:)* **You knew, didn't you?**

PAULA: *(Takes the canister, puts it in the duffel bag.)* **Every time a dog died, Dad said he would have it cremated. But he never did. Each pup went bye-bye in the car and then got a quick funeral at the Walmart dumpster. Dad kept giving Mom those cheesy canisters, but she never looked inside.** *(Pause.)* **Just how upset are you?**

SANDY: **Why? Just tell me why?**

PAULA: **You know how much cremation costs? One hundred plus for each pet, depending on weight. Dad only told me last month: too proud to ask for help when he needed it. Mom never knew, Sandy. That's what counts.**

SANDY: **So ... no ashes. The world's going crazy and now we don't even have ashes and Daddy couldn't tell me. And you weren't going to either. Were you?**

PAULA: **Not today.**

SANDY: **You know those Russian dogs in space? Some came back and some didn't — supposedly they died? Well, they're still up there. I see them in my dreams.**

PAULA: **Celebrating their fortieth birthday?**

SANDY: **FYI, time in outer space is measured differently. What now, Paula?**

PAULA: **Well, guess what, Sandy? I don't know. Unless we can** pitch yesterday into the dumpster with Louie.

SANDY: But you always know these things.

PAULA: Oh, I see. Because I'm the attorney — right? You want a prediction? Here's one: some idiots will freak. They'll beat up folks for looking weird or wired or just plain foreign.

SANDY: Because they're scared?

PAULA: Try stupid. Or ... okay, scared. I'll go with scared. Next our leaders will stomp around making threats till most of the world gets really ticked at us. Things like that. And then we'll end up fighting what a lot of folks will call a totally senseless war.

SANDY: There must be something we can do.

PAULA: You think you're the only one who has bad dreams? Everybody's scared. Mom says she was scared after World War Two. You know why? Russians had the atom bomb. Well, you know how that worked out: the world kept turning and we never got atomized. See? I'm a closet optimist.

SANDY: But what about yesterday?

PAULA: I can't change yesterday. But ... look ... before building your space ship, why don't we drive up to the cabin anyway? Then we can figure out what to do. Okay? And whatever that turns out to be, we just go do it. Day by day. Whatever it takes.

SANDY: Will it do any good?

PAULA: It can't hurt. That's all I can tell you. Come on, let's go.
(PAULA exits.)

SANDY: *(Calling after PAULA)* **Just being clear, you're humoring me about the space ship and I'm letting you do it — okay?** *(As SANDY reaches the duffel bag she lifts it without stopping and puts the bag on her shoulder.)* **Wait for us, Paula. We're coming!**

"Distended Ear Lobes"
by Katherine Burkman
from *Imaging Imogene* by Women At Play

Ruthie — Daughter, indeterminate age
Imogene — Mother, 30s–40s

This comic scene gives the actresses a clear line of development to play, with a climax that's reached in the final lines. It also presents two very clear character types, providing the performers with many choices to explore in order to move beyond the stereotype. Finally, it contains a number of indications for natural physical actions and business the actresses can use expressively. In the scene, Ruthie is sitting in a chaise with a pillow on her lap while her mother is getting dressed. Imogene dresses behind a screen, where she goes to get each new outfit she displays.

IMOGENE: *(We hear her from behind the screen, then she emerges carrying a dress that she holds up to herself as she gazes at the audience as a mirror.)* **But you said that he doesn't interest you anymore. Wouldn't you say that, if he doesn't interest you anymore, that it would be kinder not to meet him for lunch?**

RUTHIE: Well, it isn't exactly that he doesn't interest me anymore. It's that I'm not quite sure of the chemistry. Before it was all chemistry, and I didn't even think about whether he interested me. Now the chemistry is deluded and I've had time to consider whether or not he interests me, I mean as a person, that is.

IMOGENE: *(Examining herself in mirror)* **Diluted, Ruthie, not deluded. The chemistry is diluted. Deluded is what you**

are if you think there is anything in him other than chemistry to be interested in. Do you think this makes my hips look big? *(She disappears behind the screen.)*

RUTHIE: How do you know whether he's interesting or not when you haven't ever had so much as a conversation with him?

IMOGENE: *(From behind screen)* When someone is that good looking, he rarely has anything else to recommend him. *(She emerges in a new outfit.)*

RUTHIE: That's a nice sweater.

IMOGENE: I don't think the color works with this skirt. *(She disappears behind the screen.)*

RUTHIE: Anyhow, whether it's going anywhere or not, I'm having lunch with him because — now promise me not to get hysterical — he's been looking into the Peace Corps and I'm thinking about joining up with him.

IMOGENE: I think you might want to take your father's health into consideration. *(Emerges with three other tops and tries one on.)* Your joining the Peace Corps would probably give him a stroke or at the very least a mild heart attack. *(She takes off the top and throws it on the chaise, then tries on another top.)* I've actually lost four-and-a-half pounds in the last two weeks and I think my breasts have gotten bigger. And I don't understand that at all because when I went to the doctor last week and he measured me, it appears that I've shrunk a half inch, which I don't understand at all because I eat at least three Tums a day and more when I get heartburn.

RUTHIE: Mom, Dad worries about me even if he's in the same room with me and I'm curled up on the couch in front of the fire. I hate the job in the office and if you'll pardon the cliché, I want to do something worthwhile. *(RUTHIE plumps the pillow on the chaise and stretches out on it.)*

IMOGENE: Darling, don't put your shoes on the chaise, please. *(She disappears behind the screen and returns with three different pairs of shoes.)* If he worries when you're right here with us, can you imagine what he would be like if you were off saving people in some god-forsaken village in Africa? I would have to live with that, Ruthie. Why don't you just move into town and let him get used to that first? *(She puts on one of the pairs of shoes.)* **Which shoes go with this?**

RUTHIE: The white. Jacob thinks the time is now. I think the time is now.

IMOGENE: *(She has tried on one black shoe and examined it in the mirror. She decides against it and tries on a red one.)* **I'm thinking of growing my hair longer, I mean partly over my ears. I don't know if you've noticed, but the lobes of my ears are slightly distended. I think it's because of wearing those heavy earrings and not piercing my ears.**

RUTHIE: It's hard to explain but I just have this sense of myself that I haven't had in ages. I met three new guys last week and every one of them asked me for my number. Last month it was just Jacob and he didn't seem that interested and now that he's this interested it's as if it's catching and everyone seems to want to go out with me.

IMOGENE: First my mother instills her Victorian idea that only sluts and whores pierce their ears and then your father talks about mutilation and now you don't even wear earrings because I've brainwashed you and look. Do you think my ears look distended? Please don't put your shoes on my chaise.

RUTHIE: Mother, your ears are fine. You look great. Those are the shoes to wear. Will you sit down for a moment and listen to me!

IMOGENE: I am listening to you, dear. Three boys want to marry you and you persist in going out with Jacob whom nobody likes and who wants to take you to work in Calcutta. I can't find a damn thing to wear and I'm late. I'm meeting your Grandmother Rose for lunch and a concert and you know how she is if I don't look my best. I'll have to cancel. You'll have to go, darling. Just call Jacob and make it for tomorrow. *(As RUTHIE gets up, IMOGENE flings herself onto the chaise in a fetal position, covering her head with the pillow.)*

RUTHIE: Tomorrow is Monday, mother, and I'm working. Grandmother Rose is your mother. It's your darned concert series. I'm meeting Jacob for lunch. I am seriously thinking of joining the Peace Corps with Jacob. It's you who are diluted! I mean, for heaven's sake, you're shrinking! *(RUTHIE exits and then returns, grabbing the pillow and uncovering her mother's ears.)* **And I've never seen such distended ear lobes in my entire life!**

Women Behind the Walls
by Claire Braz-Valentine

1 Valdetta — Mixed race or African-American, mid-20s
2 Nicki — Mixed race or African-American, mid-20s
3
4 *This play was written from improvisation and storytelling*
5 *with the women inmates of one of California's state prisons,*
6 *and much of what is recounted here is a true-to-life incident.*
7 *The playwright explains that her drama is designed "to make us*
8 *listen, make us think of the women who are just like us except*
9 *they made a mistake and now will pay forever." In addition to*
10 *strong characterization and language skills, the scene also offers*
11 *actresses the opportunity to play a rich palette of emotions*
12 *within a very simple scene structure that is laden with conflict*
13 *and has only one turning point. The play takes place in women's*
14 *cells, and in this seriocomic scene, Nicki struggles with the*
15 *question of motherhood. She became pregnant just before she*
16 *was sentenced, and now the prison doctor has told her it is too*
17 *late for an abortion. Valdetta is her cellmate.*
18
19   *(VALDETTA is reading and NICKI comes into the room.)*
20 **NICKI:** *(Plops herself down on her bunk)* **Valdetta, can I ask you**
21   **something?**
22 **VALDETTA: Yeah, sure.**
23 **NICKI: If you had it to do over again would you have had a**
24   **child? It's too late for an abortion. Not that I had my mind**
25   **set on it. But I can't have one now. This child is going to be**
26   **born.** *(Begins crying:)* **For God's sake, Valdetta, I'm going to**
27   **be a mother. I don't know what do.**
28 **VALDETTA: Well I can't tell you what do to. This is too big a**
29   **decision for anyone to make it for you.**

NICKI: How come you never have your child visit?

VALDETTA: My child lives two hundred miles away from here. He lives in a foster home with five other foster children. *(Change — as if making excuses:)* I'm ashamed, Nicki. He's four years old and I don't want him to see his mama in prison. I could call friends. Someone would bring him. I haven't had one visitor in the two years I've been in here. I don't want to.

NICKI: I've been thinking about my baby's chances if I put it up for adoption. How many families are out there do you think that want an African American baby, born to a prostitute and her pimp? We were both on drugs when I got pregnant. *(Pause.)* You know the worst thing about growing up?

VALDETTA: No, what?

NICKI: You realize you got to make your own decisions and if you make mistakes you got no one else to blame.

VALDETTA: Honey, I got me some medals in that department. I spend my whole life blaming myself. They could have put me away for fifty years and never touch the punishment I give myself every day of my life. *(Opens her blouse and turns away from the audience.)* See these burns? I never showed no one. It's awful to look at ain't it? The flames were too high. When I walked into that room to save my baby I didn't care. The drapes blew onto my clothes. It's amazing how fire makes wind. And his little blanket was burning, and he was screaming. These marks, these awful scars and a mighty love and the blood in our veins. That's what joins my son and me. My baby was hurt, Nicki. Hurt bad.

NICKI: Oh, honey. I'm so sorry.

VALDETTA: There is no one sorrier than me. I am the sorriest excuse for a mother you ever did see. I live for the day when I can change that.

NICKI: You love David. I don't think you're a sorry excuse for a mother. I don't think they should have sent you to prison either. It's not fair. That isn't justice.

VALDETTA: No, girlfriend. That is justice. Justice is just us. Just you and just me, two black women stuck in the pen having a discourse about motherhood. Shiiiit! Just do what you can. Think about it hard. But when that baby's born, if you keep it. You're not number one anymore. It is. And it's going to stay in that number one position for a long, long time. If you want to give it up I won't hold it against you. That's your decision.

NICKI: It's just that I never had anything all my own. Oh, God! Don't you sometimes just wish you could wake up and just start life all over again?

VALDETTA: Girl, what's that saying? "This is the first day of the rest of your life?" Except you're starting out your first day pregnant, single, a convicted felon, and black! Well this is supposed to be the land of opportunity, the melting pot. Girl you're so far down in the pot you isn't got much choice but get cooked or get out.

NICKI: And for that piece of wisdom I thank you. I think you mean something like if you can't take the heat get out of the kitchen.

VALDETTA: Yeah. Whatever the hell that's supposed to mean.
(During this they begin to laugh.)

NICKI: Girl, you better talk to my hand 'cause my face don't understand.

VALDETTA: Look before you leap.

NICKI: A fool and his money are soon parted.

VALDETTA: Look who's calling the pot black! *(They are howling with laughter.)*

Two Loves and a Creature
by Gustavo Ott

Caroline — 20s–30s
Veronica — Indeterminate age

    Caroline is a veterinarian at the zoo and Veronica is her assistant. The setting is the beginning of the morning shift in the veterinary office, and Caroline has spent a sleepless night mulling over her family problems. Meanwhile the city is being rocked by terrorist bombings, and some strange fatal disease has infected the animals at the zoo. They are dying slowly one by one, and Caroline has been unable determine the nature of the disease. The scene is highly challenging. The actresses must portray normal, ordinary professional women who are suddenly caught up in very bizarre circumstances as part of their daily work and must make the best of it. Although Veronica sounds certain of what she must do, Caroline struggles to solve the problem throughout the scene — lending their dramatic relationship strong tension and interest.

CAROLINE: Night falls, hours pass, you go to bed and all you can hope is that, the next day, you'll wake up with the relief of someone leaving behind a dream. Only that night I didn't sleep. I went to work at the zoo like every day and there was my friend Veronica. ...

VERONICA: It's been a long time since I've seen you this way.

CAROLINE: What way?

VERONICA: Sad. You're sad today.

CAROLINE: Yeah, all day long I've had the feeling that it wasn't worth coming in to work.

VERONICA: You love your job, Caroline.

CAROLINE: I love it.

VERONICA: We all feel the same way. With the terrorist attacks, everyone's in that mood, gray, discouraged, that shade of something like shame and pity.

CAROLINE: What happened?

VERONICA: Thirty dead at a mall, car bomb. It was parked there and BOOM! Did you hear it? A lot of people said they heard it miles away. They're beasts. They deserve to die. I know, I don't support the death penalty, but sometimes we need it. Like for exceptions. Don't you think?

CAROLINE: I hadn't heard anything about it.

VERONICA: And you always know everything. *(She hands her a cup.)* Here, have some coffee. *(CAROLINE drinks it like water. VERONICA watches in amazement. CAROLINE pours herself some more and drinks it like juice. She pours again, but VERONICA stops her. CAROLINE realizes.)*

CAROLINE: I saw my parents yesterday.

VERONICA: I saw you by the monkey cage. Is everything okay?

CAROLINE: Yeah, everything's fine. I found out that my father made a mistake fifteen years ago.

VERONICA: Want to talk about it?

CAROLINE: No, it's all right. It was a mistake. *(Pauses like someone who will leave it at that, then suddenly:)* **My dad went to jail for killing a dog.**

VERONICA: Good God!

CAROLINE: An accident.

VERONICA: Of course. What happened?

CAROLINE: He kicked it to death.

VERONICA: What an animal! Sorry.

CAROLINE: I didn't sleep last night because I knew I'd dream about the dog.

VERONICA: So, why'd he kill it?

CAROLINE: He thought it was homosexual. *(VERONICA drops the cup. It breaks.)*

VERONICA: Maybe you better not tell me any more. Do you

want to take the day off, go home? There's nothing for you to do here today.

CAROLINE: Yeah, you're right. I better go. *(Preparing to leave.)* Remember you've got to keep a special eye on the black goat today; it could be her day. Don't forget to talk to the students. So they won't let anyone touch the babies. We're expecting two goats, alive and kicking. And tell them not to forget the mandrill's vaccination. And check the bird cage, to see if they're getting better.

VERONICA: Okay. Okay. Go. Everything's under control. We don't need you here today.

CAROLINE: Maybe it's a virus.

VERONICA: Go on, get out of here. You look beat. Whether it's a virus or whatever, nothing ever happens to the birds. They're the strongest of all.

CAROLINE: Parrots are like lions.

VERONICA: They get sick less than the elephants.

CAROLINE: And they get themselves in all kind of trouble ... ! *(Leaving.)* Don't forget to let the orangutan out.

VERONICA: I'll take care of it. Goodbye. *(CAROLINE is about to leave, but comes back. VERONICA looks at her, knowing what's coming.)*

CAROLINE: What do you think I should do?

VERONICA: About ... ?

CAROLINE: Yesterday.

VERONICA: You can't do anything about terrorists, Caroline. Wish them dead or that their car bomb blows up on them, or their plastic explosives go off, their automatic weapons jam and backfire, that they make a mistake and kill each other. Or their families, let their families die, too.

CAROLINE: Veronica!

VERONICA: I'm sick of them!

CAROLINE: I meant about my father. What should I do?

VERONICA: That was years ago.

CAROLINE: I just found out yesterday.

VERONICA: I don't interfere in family matters. Your father's your father. So off to bed with you, and to work with me. And as for the terrorists, death. See you tomorrow.
(VERONICA disappears in the dark. CAROLINE remains Onstage. She takes her bag. Walks.)

CAROLINE: I left the office, but I didn't go home. I went walking around the zoo. Everything was normal. Not many visitors. I stopped at the bird cage, because they're very sick and we don't know why. They have such a strange disease. So unusual. They don't fly. They don't want to or can't. We've run every possible test, but we didn't find any pathology. They're just there, with no desire to fly. And all I do is watch them every morning, completely powerless, because I was used to being able to do something for them, and now, well, now I can't.

Scenes for Men and Women

Guides
by Josh Overton

1. Leanne — Teens
2. Luke — Teens
3. Danny — Teens

The scene takes place in Leanne's bedroom where she's getting ready for her date to the dance with Danny. She's speaking to herself at her dressing table when Luke bursts in. The scene is rich in subtext that reveals manipulation, discoveries, uncertainty, impulsiveness, and tender feelings. Although the scene elicits great sympathy for Danny and Leanne, the actor portraying Luke should not play the character simply as a "bad guy" who tries to bully Leanne's new boyfriend. Luke can become much more interesting if the actor also reveals some of the character's vulnerability, embarrassment, and pain.

LEANNE: *(To her reflection)* **What do you think of this dress? Too formal? Nah. You like it? I love it.** *(She busies herself with makeup and hair, talking to her reflection.)* **This is all so scary. What if he doesn't show up? What would I do then? He is coming, right?** *(Silence.)* **He's coming. I know he's coming. I can feel it.** *(LUKE barges in.)*

LUKE: **You can feel what? Hey there, sunshine. What are you all dressed up for?**

LEANNE: **Luke! What are you doing here?**

LUKE: **I heard you were in a bit of trouble, so I came over right away.**

LEANNE: **Trouble? I'm not in trouble. ...**

LUKE: **Oh, yes you are. You are about to have your heart**

broken, and I'm not going to let that happen.
LEANNE: Luke, please. ...
LUKE: What, do you think you and Danny are going to live happily ever after and all that? Huh? Tell me honestly. Do you *really* believe that can happen?
LEANNE: *(Confused)* Well, I think so. ...
LUKE: Look at me! See? You don't believe it! There is no fairy tale. There is no happy ending. There is no happily ever after.
LEANNE: *(Crying)* Oh, Luke. Why did you have to come here?
LUKE: Because someone had to speak sense to you.
LEANNE: But Danny really likes me!
LUKE: Oh, please. Mr. Stanford? Not likely. He'll be gone in a few months, off to the university, leaving you here to go to the city college. How long do you see that lasting? Happily ever after? Not even.
LEANNE: But he believes in me.
LUKE: What, I don't? Danny doesn't believe in you. He's just playing with you. Nobody else believes in you, Leanne.
LEANNE: I believe in me. *(Beat.)*
LUKE: I see.
LEANNE: I want you to go away, Luke. I want you to go away and never come back.
LUKE: I have a car outside, parked and ready to go to California.
LEANNE: What? You don't own a car.
LUKE: My ... uh ... uncle gave it to me. He wants me to go start my life in California right away. Come with me. We can be in California in a couple of days. I know a guy there who can get you an agent.
LEANNE: Oh, Luke. ...
LUKE: Come on, grab your things. Let's go!
LEANNE: What about Danny? I can't. I'm going to stay here. I'm going to the dance with Danny.
LUKE: What if Danny doesn't show up? What if he stands you up?

1 LEANNE: He wouldn't do that.
2 LUKE: Are you sure?
3 LEANNE: *(Unsure)* **Yes.**
4 LUKE: What time does the dance start?
5 LEANNE: At six.
6 LUKE: What time is it now?
7 LEANNE: *(Looking at her watch)* **Six-fifteen.**
8 LUKE: He's not coming, Leanne. You can't trust him. I'm the
9   only person you can trust. Come with me. Let's go start
10   our life all over. Come on!
11 LEANNE: I can't do that.
12 LUKE: Yes, you can, it's easy. Just throw some clothes into a
13   suitcase. Let's go!
14 LEANNE: *(Beginning to cave-in)* **Where would we stay?**
15 LUKE: Don't worry about it, I have it all worked out. *(LEANNE*
16   *reluctantly begins to pack a suitcase.)*
17 LEANNE: Luke, I'm scared.
18 LUKE: I know, Leanne. Hurry up and pack. We'll be in
19   California before you know it.
20 LEANNE: *(To the heavens)* **Is this what I am supposed to do?**
21   *(DANNY knocks twice on the door.)* **Danny? Come in!**
22   *(DANNY enters, dressed for the dance.)*
23 DANNY: Hi! I'm so sorry I'm late, but somebody slashed the
24   tires of my mom's car. ... *(He sees LUKE.)* **Oh, hi, Luke.**
25 LUKE: Danny. What are you doing here?
26 LEANNE: Don't, Luke.
27 LUKE: I asked you a question, smart-boy.
28 DANNY: Hey, I'm just here to take Leanne to the dance.
29 LEANNE: Luke, you need to go.
30 LUKE: Remember what I told you a couple days ago, Danny?
31   Don't even look at my girl.
32 DANNY: Which girl are you talking about? Genie? Sarah? Leanne?
33 LUKE: Watch your mouth, smart-boy.
34 LEANNE: What does he mean, which girl? Are you going with
35   Genie and Sarah, too?

1 DANNY: Yeah, he is.
2 LUKE: I warned you. *(LUKE hits DANNY, knocking him to the*
3   *floor. LEANNE rushes to DANNY.)*
4 LEANNE: Danny!
5 LUKE: Come on, Leanne. Let's go. Grab your stuff and let's go.
6   Hollywood is waiting.
7 LEANNE: Get out. Get out. *(Screaming:)* Get out!
8 LUKE: Fine. *(LUKE exits in a huff. LEANNE helps DANNY to his*
9   *feet.)*
10 LEANNE: Oh, Danny. I am so sorry. Are you okay?
11 DANNY: I couldn't be better.
12 LEANNE: You're kidding.
13 DANNY: Nope. You chose me. Luke could hit me a hundred
14   more times and it would be worth it.
15 LEANNE: You are going to have the worst black eye.
16 DANNY: I have something for you.
17 LEANNE: Danny! Sit down!
18 DANNY: I'm fine! Really! *(He picks up a bag that he dropped*
19   *when he was hit.)* This is for you.
20 LEANNE: You didn't have to buy me anything.
21 DANNY: I didn't. This used to be mine. I wanted you to have it.
22   *(LEANNE opens the bag and removes a stuffed bumblebee.)*
23 LEANNE: *(Confused)* Thank you ... it's very sweet.
24 DANNY: His name is Leaf.
25 LEANNE: Leaf?
26 DANNY: B-Leaf. It was my own little reminder to have belief in
27   myself.
28 LEANNE: You're kidding me, right?
29 DANNY: No, not at all. *(Beat. LEANNE struggles with the*
30   *corniness of this.)*
31 LEANNE: B-Leaf. I love it. Thank you so much, Danny.
32 DANNY: Can you do me a favor?
33 LEANNE: Sure.
34 DANNY: Call me Dan. I've always hated being called Danny.
35 LEANNE: Sure thing ... Dan. I guess you can call me B-anne!

(They both laugh at this awful joke.)

DANNY: Nah. I like Leanne a whole lot more. *(Pause for this to sink in.)* **You ready to go?**

LEANNE: Yeah. Let's go dance like geeks. *(Exit laughing.)*

How His Bride Came to Abraham
by Karen Sunde

1   Abe — 20s
2   Sabra — 20s
3
4   *Abe is a lone Israeli infantryman wounded on a patrol who*
5   *encounters a young Arab woman, Sabra. She leads him to*
6   *refuge in a small hut, but he's unaware that she's a Palestinian*
7   *trying to go home to Jerusalem, who will strap explosives to*
8   *herself tomorrow, infiltrate Israeli territory, and expect to die.*
9   *She's told him that she was just out picking apples when she*
10 *ran into him. Abe awaits his patrol, who will soon return to*
11 *pick him up, but for the moment he and Sabra share an*
12 *uneasy, mutually suspicious time together, warily getting to*
13 *know each other. They have just finished eating.*
14
15 **ABE:** What do your parents say about you?
16 **SABRA:** *(Averting her gaze)* **My parents.**
17 **ABE:** Yes. Is this — what you're up to — proper behavior for a
18   fine young Arab of good. ... *(He stops himself, seeing she's*
19   *upset.)*
20 **SABRA:** *(Matter-of-factly)* **I don't have any.**
21 **ABE:** No parents?
22 **SABRA:** *(Looks at him)* **It was a bomb. In a car.**
23 **ABE:** And that's why you don't exist?
24 **SABRA:** *(Shakes her head, vaguely)* **No. I never existed.**
25 **ABE:** Sabra. Your brothers. You said ...
26 **SABRA:** **They weren't really my brothers. They're Um Sa'ad's sons.**
27 **ABE:** *(Glad to have an answer he can translate)* **Um Sa'ad. The**
28   **mother of Sa'ad. She ... raised you?** *(SABRA looks at him*
29   *with quiet eyes.)*

ABE: *(Satisfied to finally have a clear answer)* **Well. That's something.**

SABRA: How many Arabs have you killed?

ABE: None. None! Sabra, listen. I asked for this. I transferred here, out of Israel, so I wouldn't wind up killing children! I don't like this. You think I want to kill someone? I don't hate Arabs. I only want to live in peace. But they keep on coming to kill us. And I'll tell you, it's not like you think. They've got no chance here. No chance to win. To even fight. I've seen it work. One night on ambush, I crawled back to the APC, the tank, and inside, they're watching with a night-scope, on a screen, like a video cartoon! And there come the stick creatures. They show up on the screen because they're alive out there, they're warm, they're moving – not even close, a whole kilometer away! And because it's night, we don't ask – we just fire. We fire, several rounds, and every shell seeks warmth, and bursts itself in flesh. We watch. In silence ... the creatures falter on the screen. No shrieks. Nothing. The stick shapes just begin to fade, getting dimmer as their warmth is lost, until they blank out, blending with the screen, completely cold. *(Pause.)* No. I've never *seen* anyone die.

SABRA: *(Darkly)* **Lucky.**

ABE: *(Shouts)* **I'm protecting the border, farmers two kilometers from here! Am I allowed to defend my home?!** *(His outburst strikes her strangely. She looks at him, open, like a child.)*

SABRA: Home. Yes. *(Beat.)* **What's it like?**

ABE: I ... what?

SABRA: Your home.

ABE: *My* home.

SABRA: Yes. You have one?

ABE: Of course!

SABRA: What's it like?

ABE: It's. ... What do you mean?

SABRA: A house. A farm?

ABE: Just a house. A ...

SABRA: On a hill?

ABE: Well ... Yes, a hill.

SABRA: Is there a tree?

ABE: What are you after?

SABRA: It's old, isn't it?

ABE: *(Amused)* I don't understand.

SABRA: *(Asking him to imagine himself there)* You're at home. You see your mother. Your father. A rug by the door. A picture of your sister and you — but younger.

ABE: *(Seeing his home)* Yes. ...

SABRA: Are you afraid?

ABE: At home? No.

SABRA: No one is?

ABE: My gramma.

SABRA: She's afraid?

ABE: My mother was born in a camp ... in Germany.

SABRA: A camp? With no sewer?

ABE: No, I think ... I think they had a sewer.

SABRA: She was afraid.

ABE: Yes.

SABRA: So, then, in the camp with her baby — your gramma had no home.

ABE: No, then she didn't. And later. ...

SABRA: Did someone take it? Did she fight?

ABE: It wasn't exactly. ...

SABRA: You have to fight. It's your home.

ABE: Yes.

SABRA: If they come in the night. Where it's safe. Where your mother holds you. Where you go to sleep.

ABE: *(Alarmed)* Sabra. What is it? What happened? *(She stops, looks at him, her eyes hurting.)* How old were you.

SABRA: How old?

ABE: When your parents were killed.

SABRA: Old. Plenty old.

ABE: How many years?

SABRA: *(Pause. Without emotion:)* **Eight.** *(ABE swallows hard, not knowing what to say, covers his readiness to cry with whimsy, wanting to make her smile.)*

ABE: And here you are ... apple hunting — a spirit in the woods, who's snatched me, this unsuspecting soldier, a spirit ... who doesn't even exist. *(She only looks at him.)* **Does Um Sa'ad tell stories?**

SABRA: Stories?

ABE: Yes. Good stories.

SABRA: Not now.

ABE: But before.

SABRA: Sometimes. About a bird.

ABE: Tell me. *(She looks far away.)* **Don't go.**

SABRA: I'm not.

ABE: Yes, you did. You raised your wings.

SABRA: No.

ABE: You left. You tried. *(She looks at him.)* **You're my captive here. You have to stay in my good graces. I want to see this hand.** *(He takes her hand, turns it to look at her palm.)* **Aha. You know what I see here? In this line here.** *(Tracing it:)* **This life line. ...**

SABRA: I don't have any.

ABE: Ah ah ah, let me look. What I see is a good hand, a strong one. It ... it dreams. It feels ... many things. It needs to build a strong life. I have hold of it here, you see? It does ... exist. *(She looks at him. Her mouth opens, but no sound comes out. Suddenly, she weeps, hard, bends over weeping. He is startled, nearly weeps himself. He puts his arm around her. She sobs, clings to his arm.)* **Don't. Don't, don't, Sabra. It's all right.** *(He leans over, kisses her hair. Then kisses her cheek. She breathes deep, catching her breath, realizes what's happening, raises her head to look in his face, questioningly.)* **I'm sorry. I. ...** *(He stops speaking, goes on looking at her as* *she gazes at him. Then, suddenly she leans forward and kisses him on the mouth, slowly, then pulls back again to look at him. He smiles.)* **Well. Thank you. That ... I'm sure that did happen. So, my Shabbat angel, tell me your story.**

Blue Girl
by Deborah Aita

1 Tiffany — Mixed race (black mother, white father), 18, singer
2 Charlie — Black, Tiffany's boyfriend, musician
3 Marcia — Black, Tiffany's friend, pianist
4
5 *This amusing scene begins as a three-character piece and*
6 *then concludes as a two-character love scene. It has a number*
7 *of "theatrical" moments in the first section, and then develops*
8 *into a sincere love scene before reaching a playful conclusion*
9 *with a joke at the end about the age of Tiffany's mother. What*
10 *makes the scene even more interesting is that the stage*
11 *directions indicating pauses and moments of embarrassment*
12 *probably occur in those places where such emotions would*
13 *naturally arise between the actors playing the scene regardless*
14 *of their "dramatic" relationships.*
15
16 (CHARLIE *enters to find* TIFFANY *and* MARCIA. *He is black,*
17 *a similar age as they, and dressed in casual, baggy clothes,*
18 *baseball cap, etc. He is staggering, out of breath and seems to*
19 *have been hurt.)*
20 **CHARLIE:** Oh God! Oh God! You won't believe. ...
21 **TIFFANY:** Charlie!
22 **MARCIA:** What is it Charlie?
23 **TIFFANY:** Are you hurt? (CHARLIE *falls to the ground and the*
24 *girls rush over to kneel by him.)*
25 **CHARLIE:** I can't breathe.
26 **MARCIA:** Oh my God, what is it?
27 **TIFFANY:** Loosen his shirt.
28 **MARCIA:** Where does it hurt, Charlie?
29 **CHARLIE:** They ... they said they were going to kill me.

TIFFANY: Who?

MARCIA: Are you in trouble?

CHARLIE: Three white boys.

TIFFANY: What?

MARCIA: What did they do?

CHARLIE: *(Groaning)* **Oh God!**

TIFFANY: I'm calling the police.

CHARLIE: Wait!

MARCIA: You poor brave boy!

CHARLIE: Tiffany! Just ... just, hold my hand. *(MARCIA takes his hand instead.)*

MARCIA: Of course Charlie, you're so brave.

CHARLIE: Tiffany, help me!

TIFFANY: What can I do?

CHARLIE: My head! *(TIFFANY puts her hand on Charlie's forehead.)*

CHARLIE: Ah! Your hand is so cool.

MARCIA: Oh Charlie, tell us what happened.

CHARLIE: Aaah, my stomach! *(He takes TIFFANY's other hand and places it on his stomach.)*

CHARLIE: Aaah!

TIFFANY: *(Suspiciously)* **Where exactly does it hurt, Charlie?**

CHARLIE: Everywhere.

TIFFANY: Good, so if I hit you here it'll hurt a lot. *(She hits him hard.)*

CHARLIE: Ooowww!

MARCIA: Tiffany, what are you doing? *(CHARLIE groans dramatically. TIFFANY stands up.)*

TIFFANY: Cut it out, Charlie. I don't believe you.

CHARLIE: *(Sitting up)* **Don't you?**

MARCIA: Charlie!

TIFFANY: Can't you ever take anything seriously?

CHARLIE: I take you seriously.

MARCIA: Charlie, how could you!

CHARLIE: Got you going there, didn't I, Marcia?

TIFFANY: It's not a joking matter.
MARCIA: That was a real mean trick.
CHARLIE: You think I'd let three white boy punks scare me?
MARCIA: Well they might have been big guys.
CHARLIE: There'd have to be at least ten to scare me!
MARCIA: Mister Macho!
TIFFANY: You're such a big kid.
CHARLIE: Hey girls, it was a joke.
MARCIA: Pretty sick joke, if you ask me.
TIFFANY: Don't play with people's emotions, Charlie.
CHARLIE: *(Suddenly serious)* Well you're playing with mine.
   (TIFFANY and CHARLIE stare at each other in silence for a moment and then both turn away. MARCIA is stuck in the middle.)
MARCIA: *(Singing)* I wonder what's the matter? *(TIFFANY waits a moment before joining in.)*
TIFFANY: *(Singing)* Oh-o, Lord.
MARCIA: *(Singing)* I wonder what's the matter with this poor boy's head! *(MARCIA playfully smacks Charlie on the head. They all laugh. The tension eases.)*
MARCIA: I'm starved. You got anything to eat?
CHARLIE: No.
MARCIA: I'll go to the corner and get us something. Any orders?
CHARLIE: *(Together)* I've eaten.
TIFFANY: *(Together)* No thanks.
MARCIA: *(Knowingly)* Well, I'll just leave you two ... alone!
   (MARCIA exits. Another silence. CHARLIE looks at the photo of Carla.)
TIFFANY: That really wasn't funny, Charlie.
CHARLIE: No, you're right. It was cheap.
TIFFANY: Especially when you're twenty minutes late.
CHARLIE: Only twenty minutes?
TIFFANY: Why don't you take anything seriously?
CHARLIE: You said that before, Tiff. *(They're embarrassed again. Silence.)*

1 TIFFANY: My Dad says we can't rehearse down here any more.
2 CHARLIE: What!
3 TIFFANY: He just can't bear to hear me sing.
4 CHARLIE: What are you talking about?
5 TIFFANY: You know how he hates me being involved in music.
6 CHARLIE: No, I don't know. It's one thing to want you to study
7   more, but that's crazy, with all this space doing nothing
8   and a daughter who can sing the birds out of the sky!
9 TIFFANY: Charlie!
10 CHARLIE: Well, you know!
11 TIFFANY: *(Teasingly)* I didn't know you could be so poetic.
12 CHARLIE: Poetic! Me! No, no, no. I'm a wild-child. I'm dangerous!
13 TIFFANY: You! Dangerous? *(TIFFANY walks towards CHARLIE.*
14   *He stands still and waits.)*
15 CHARLIE: Better stay away from me. I'll eat you alive!
16 TIFFANY: Really!
17 CHARLIE: Yeah!
18 TIFFANY: Yeah?
19 CHARLIE: Yeah. *(TIFFANY stands very close to Charlie.)*
20 TIFFANY: Show me. *(They kiss passionately.)* We should have
21   done that a long time ago.
22 CHARLIE: Too right!
23 TIFFANY: I'm sorry I was angry at you.
24 CHARLIE: That's okay. I'm sorry I was late.
25 TIFFANY: That's okay. *(They laugh.)*
26 TIFFANY: Hey, what am I talking about. It's not okay. We've got
27   the show tomorrow. You're late and Marcia's thinking
28   about her belly!
29 CHARLIE: And we've got no rehearsal space.
30 TIFFANY: What am I going to do about my Dad?
31 CHARLIE: Maybe he'd change his mind if he heard how good
32   you are.
33 TIFFANY: That's not the point. He can't stand to hear me sing
34   because it reminds him too much of my mother.
35 CHARLIE: But that was years ago. You were only a baby when

she died.

TIFFANY: He never got over it. It happened so suddenly, see? There was no time to get used to the idea, no long illness or anything, just a call from the hospital to come and identify the body.

CHARLIE: Do you remember anything?

TIFFANY: No. Dad never wanted to talk about it. *(Pause.)* You know my grandmother died young too? Well, Dad thinks there's some kind of connection.

CHARLIE: I wouldn't put him down as the superstitious type.

TIFFANY: Yeah, well don't believe everything you see. He may seem all hard and businesslike, but he's a real softy underneath. He wants me to break the grand tradition of early deaths, and that means not becoming a singer.

CHARLIE: It is kind of weird to have two generations, both singers, dying so young. *(Looking at the portrait:)* How old was she, when she died?

TIFFANY: She was 45.

"Competition"
by Elizabeth Nash
from *It's Academic* by Women At Play

1. Lucy — Mid-20s
2. Will — Mid-20s

Lucy and Will are young graduate students, working at their relationship and sharing an apartment. Will is packing his suitcase on the bed, and Lucy is nearby in a chair, innocently reading. The scene gives the actors excellent opportunities for playing emotional reactions, discoveries, and a clear character development from beginning to end. It also offers actors a wide choice of physical actions. The humor can operate on many levels, as Will slowly comes to recognize some of the "masculine" assumptions on which he's based this relationship.

WILL: Lucy, have you seen my black belt with the silver buckle?

LUCY: *(Looks up from book)* **Well, let's see, the last time I wore it.** *(Pause.)*

WILL: What?

LUCY: I said, Why don't you try the floor. That's where you usually store your stuff.

WILL: Very funny, Lucy. Oh, here it is. *(He retrieves his belt from floor and puts it on. Takes book from LUCY and presents himself.)* So, what do you think?

LUCY: You can dress yourself. Very good. *(She retrieves book and continues to read.)*

WILL: Come on, Lucy. What's the matter with you? Ever since I got back, it's been nonstop sarcasm. For the umpteenth time, I'm sorry you couldn't come along, but you know how these trips are. Now I'm asking for your opinion. Is this shirt appropriate, or should I wear one of those collarless ones?

LUCY: Appropriate for what?

WILL: Come on, Lucy! You know for what. For the conference – the meeting with Virginia, to convince her I'm the one and only choice for the assistantship. Of course, it's almost totally academic – I've got it sewn up anyway; I have essentially no credible competition, no reason to worry after this last stint of incredibly good work I've –

LUCY: *(Still looking down at her book)* **You do.**

WILL: Do what?

LUCY: Have competition.

WILL: No, I don't.

LUCY: Yes, you do.

WILL: This is rapidly ceasing to be amusing, Lucy. We are speaking about the vital stepping stone in my entire academic career here, the goal toward which I ... and you ... have been working for the past two years! Ever since you moved in with me. Who could possibly compete with me?

LUCY: *(Looking down at her book as if reading)* **Me.**

WILL: You?

LUCY: That's right, me.

WILL: You've got to be kidding.

LUCY: Oh, thank you, Will. Thank you so much for entirely dismissing my accomplishments, my stature as a scholar. ...

WILL: But ... I thought we agreed ...

LUCY: We didn't agree on anything, Will. You assumed.

WILL: But you implied. ...

LUCY: Pardon my forgetfulness, but when did we sign a non-compete contract? I love this work as much as you do; I think I can make a real contribution because I happen to care about my students. This assistantship makes as much sense as a next step – a *crucial* step – for me as it does for you.

WILL: This is just unbelievable ... in fact, I *don't* believe you. I don't know why you're doing this. If it's true, what's the evidence? Give me one single, solitary shred of real, hard evidence. ...

LUCY: You were gone a long time, Will. Hard to keep in touch. Impossible to hear everything that's said ...

WILL: Said? What was said? What did you hear, Lucy? What did she say about me?

LUCY: As I said, Will, you were a long way from here. *(Pause)* And even when you're around, you miss stuff.

Can't Believe It
by R.N. Sandberg

1 Ron — Teens
2 Kathryn — Teens
3 Teresa — Teens
4
5   *Ron, Kathryn, and Teresa are all high school students. This*
6 *scene takes place at school, just before Ron's drama rehearsal.*
7 *Ron is trying to cover up his partying activities before Kathryn*
8 *because they have a date planned this weekend, but she*
9 *catches him in a lie just as Ron's new girlfriend, Teresa,*
10 *arrives. There is a lot of comedy here, and the actors can play*
11 *a rich subtext because the spoken dialog expresses only the*
12 *tips of the emotional icebergs that lurk beneath the surface.*
13 *Additionally, the actors should look to develop contradictory*
14 *motives in each of their characters because the scene can call*
15 *for more than a simple "old girlfriend-new girlfriend"*
16 *interpretation. For example, does Ron really want to break up*
17 *with Kathryn, and vice versa? And how are Teresa's emotions*
18 *torn when she arrives and discovers Ron with Kathryn?*
19
20 RON: Man, am I glad to see you.
21 KATHRYN: You never called me back.
22 RON: You don't know what I been goin' through. Golding lost
23   my paper and I've been bustin' butt all weekend.
24 KATHRYN: Oh yeah? Guess things didn't turn out like you
25   thought.
26 RON: Look, I'm sorry I didn't call you back. Really. You get
27   your dress? You don't know how I'm looking forward to
28   Saturday.
29 KATHRYN: I got it.

RON: You have any time to start studying for History? D'you do up your study guides and all?

KATHRYN: You're unbelievable.

RON: What?

KATHRYN: I'm not lendin' ya anything, Ron.

RON: Who's askin'?

KATHRYN: I know the way your mind works.

RON: One of the fringe benefits of intimacy, right?

KATHRYN: How was Mike's party?

RON: Boring. I left early.

KATHRYN: Was that before or after you got it on with the freshman?

RON: What? No. No way.

KATHRYN: Yeah?

RON: You don't understand. She just jumped me. She was like a stalker. I mean, nothing happened. I just got out of there. You think I'd — when I'm with you?

KATHRYN: And you expect me to believe that? *(TERESA enters.)*

RON: Kath, we know each other.

KATHRYN: Exactly. Find yourself someone else to dump on.
(She exits.)

RON: Kath? Kathryn?! Oh, hey. How you doin'?

TERESA: I'm sorry. I didn't mean to —

RON: Nah, it's okay. No biggie. My life just went down the toilet. *(He laughs.)*

TERESA: I'm sorry.

RON: Whatta ya gonna do, huh? Hey, did you end up okay after the party?

TERESA: Yeah. It was all right.

RON: I was worried.

TERESA: You were?

RON: You were really upset. I mean, Raz is harmless, but I can see how he could scare you.

TERESA: It wasn't him so much. It was more me.

RON: Yeah?

1 TERESA: It's nothing. It's not really that interesting.
2 RON: Sure it is. I can't believe we're in class together and we've
3   never really hung out. Must be hard bein' the only
4   freshman in the class.
5 TERESA: It's not bad. I know it's stupid but I like history.
6 RON: Me, too. All the politics, the maneuvering. You must
7   really know your stuff.
8 TERESA: Not really.
9 RON: Come on.
10 TERESA: I'm okay.
11 RON: More than okay. Hey, look, are you goin' right home or
12   you gonna hang out? Cause – well, I promised Ms. Miller
13   I'd do this drama thing, but if you're gonna be around,
14   maybe we could chill.
15 TERESA: Sure.
16 RON: Okay. See ya in a few. *(He exits.)*
17 TERESA: I think I'm gonna pass out my heart is beating so fast.
18   I'm gonna hyperventilate. Breathe. Breathe. He's really
19   interested. I can't believe it.

Halls of Horror
by Josh Overton

1 Jake — Teens
2 Anna — Teens
3
4 *Jake and Anna are in their high school, confined to a room*
5 *with their teacher on account of a possible chemical explosion*
6 *that is threatening their city. The scene begins with Anna*
7 *trying to cheer up Jake, who has recently broken up with his*
8 *girlfriend, Gretchen. But their conversation quickly reveals*
9 *the troubled subtext of Anna's own relationship with Jason, a*
10 *boy who has disappeared from school and is probably now*
11 *dead. By the time the scene concludes, the roles have been*
12 *reversed: it is now Jake who is reassuring Anna, and Anna who*
13 *discovers how astutely Jake has been able to pinpoint the*
14 *source of her worry. The scene is deceptively ordinary and*
15 *challenges the actors to play fully all the discoveries, reversals,*
16 *and surprises that the relationship provides.*
17
18 JAKE: How are you holding up, Anna?
19 ANNA: I'm okay. I guess. I just can't believe all of this is
20   happening, you know?
21 JAKE: Yeah. It's like a bad dream.
22 ANNA: I don't want to talk about it, okay?
23 JAKE: Yeah, okay.
24 ANNA: Let's talk about something else. Um ... football. You're
25   on the team, right?
26 JAKE: Yeah.
27 ANNA: What position do you play?
28 JAKE: I'm the center.
29 ANNA: You like playing center?

JAKE: Yeah ... it's okay. *(ANNA knows that this conversation is going nowhere. She tries a different approach.)*

ANNA: Do you have a girlfriend?

JAKE: Nah. I did ... but she broke up with me last week. She didn't think I was smart enough.

ANNA: Man, that sucks.

JAKE: Yeah. I really miss her sometimes, you know? We had lots of fun.

ANNA: What was ... what is her name?

JAKE: It was Gretchen.

ANNA: *(Stifling her laughter)* Gretchen?

JAKE: *(Laughing)* Yeah. God, what a messed-up name. She was really cool, though, you know. You'd think that with a name like Gretchen she'd be this whacked-out girl. But she wasn't. Not at all.

ANNA: What was she into?

JAKE: Football. She came to all my games. She would tell me all the stuff I was doing wrong. She even taught me how to hike it way back on punts. I kept messing it up, hiking the ball over our punters' heads. Gretchen would just say, "Relax. Don't grip the ball so hard and just toss it to him like it's no big deal." It worked.

ANNA: She sounds cool.

JAKE: Yeah. She was. She was real cool. *(Uncomfortable silence.)*

ANNA: I'm going to miss Jason.

JAKE: Anna, we don't know —

ANNA: He's gone, Jake. I know that. *(Beat.)* Things are going to be different from now on, aren't they? *(JAKE nods.)* I guess we just have to move on ... forget where we came from.

JAKE: Don't say that, Anna. We can't forget where we came from. I'm not going to forget Gretchen or football or any of this. How can I? And how can you? You and Jason were like the ... I don't know ... king and queen of this school, you know?

ANNA: King and Queen of Scary High?

JAKE: You know what I mean. Everybody knew you two.

Everybody wanted to be like you two. You guys had something that none of us could have. Don't forget that, Anna. Don't ever forget that.

ANNA: I think Gretchen was the stupid one.

JAKE: What? Why do you say that?

ANNA: She didn't know how smart you really are.

Your Molotov Kisses
by Gustavo Ott

1   Daniel — Late 20s
2   Victoria — Late 20s
3
4   *Daniel and Victoria are young, married professionals who*
5   *are working at their relationship and considering having*
6   *children. He is an attorney and she an anchorwoman. This*
7   *evening a package was delivered to their home containing*
8   *Victoria's backpack that was stolen from her twelve years*
9   *previously. She and Daniel eagerly unpack the parcel — and*
10 *discover more than either of them had bargained for. The*
11 *scene is filled with surprises — particularly for Daniel — and*
12 *contains numerous opportunities for physical business. The*
13 *scene also offers excellent opportunities for each actor to play*
14 *a range of emotions from humor to horror, to build strong*
15 *character development, and to play twists, turns, and*
16 *discoveries from beginning to end.*
17
18 **VICTORIA: Georgia!**
19 **DANIEL: Georgia what?**
20 **VICTORIA: My puppy dog, Georgia!**
21 **DANIEL: It looks more like a rat that just climbed out of the**
22   **sewer. ...**
23 **VICTORIA: My sweet Georgia. I thought I'd lost you. ...**
24 **DANIEL: A present from your first love?** *(During the following*
25   *lines, DANIEL pulls things from the bag. More dirty clothes.*
26   *Travel items, post cards, makeup, tapes, etc.)*
27 **VICTORIA:** *(Winds Georgia up, who plays the tune "Twinkle,*
28   *Twinkle, Little Star.")* **She still plays.**
29 **DANIEL: Music for retards. It suits you.**

VICTORIA: I slept with her in my cradle, I'll have you know. My dad gave her to me when I was little, I can't even remember when. But she was always with me, I couldn't sleep without hugging her. Georgia was so important to me that, for a long time, her name was another word for sleep. Daddy would say, "Vicky, it's time to Georgia" and I would jump right in bed, with a smile, to hear *(Sings:)* "twinkle, twinkle, little star...."

DANIEL: If all this means we have to sleep with her, I'm telling you she at least needs a bath first.

VICTORIA: You know she became my imaginary friend.

DANIEL: *(Shouts)* Wanted: one psychiatrist, must have own cage, make house calls. Patient desperate.

VICTORIA: My sweet Georgia. *(As if speaking to her imaginary friend:)* I've got so much to tell you! And you me. It's a good thing you came back to me. I'll never lose you again.

DANIEL: If she answers, I'm calling the FBI, but direct to the office of the X Files. *(He finds something important.)* Victoria: you're not going to believe it! *(DANIEL pulls out the Canon camera.)*

VICTORIA: No way!

DANIEL: It looks fine.

VICTORIA: Impossible!

DANIEL: It's a little out of date, but it's a good lens. *(Looks it over.)* These are still expensive. All the equipment is here. Nothing's broken, it's all fine.

VCTORIA: Let me see.

DANIEL: You took pictures.

VICTORIA: What?

DANIEL: There's a 24-exposure roll in here and you shot 13. *(She checks. She pushes a button by accident and the camera begins to make noise.)*

VICTORIA: Can the battery still be working?

DANIEL: You're ruining the film.

VICTORIA: You think?

DANIEL: I'm not stupid.

VICTORIA: I didn't do it on purpose, stop being paranoid.

DANIEL: You know what you're doing with that, Victoria. You don't make mistakes with a camera in your hands. *(But he also knows how to use it. He stops it. Opens it. Takes out the roll of film.)* I wonder what pictures are in here.

VICTORIA: That's in the past.

DANIEL: I'll get them developed tomorrow.

VICTORIA: There's nothing. ...

DANIEL: If there's nothing, then what do you care?

VICTORIA: Do what you want! *(DANIEL pulls something wrapped as a present from the box.)*

DANIEL: What's this?

VICTORIA: What?

DANIEL: A present.

VICTORIA: It must be for — *(DANIEL reads the tag. His tone and face change.)*

DANIEL: Victoria —

VICTORIA: Yes?

DANIEL: *(Reading)* "For my wife Victoria, on her birthday. No hard feelings. I love you, Ramani Prianka. *(VICTORIA goes stock still.)* What ... what ... what is this?

VICTORIA: I. ...

DANIEL: My wife Victoria? You?

VICTORIA: Daniel ... that was ... for. ...

DANIEL: What Victoria is this? You? Who is Ramani Prianka?

VICTORIA: This ... well ... I ... there was another Victoria in —

DANIEL: You were married?

VICTORIA: It's ancient history.

DANIEL: It was twelve years ago, I know that. You were married?

VICTORIA: It was in —

DANIEL: You were married?

VICTORIA: I was just a girl of —

DANIEL: Excuse me?

VICTORIA: It was twelve years ago, Daniel, twelve years ago.

DANIEL: And what happened?

VICTORIA: It was a fling ... it didn't work out, of course.

DANIEL: But you got married?

VICTORIA: More or less.

DANIEL: *(Blows up)* **What do you mean more or less? Did you get married or didn't you, Victoria?**

VICTORIA: *(Frightened)* **Yes, I got married.** *(DANIEL looks like he'd seen a ghost.)*

DANIEL: You never told me. ... Never. ... Never ...

VICTORIA: Because it was a long time ago and it only lasted a few months, Daniel. I was a kid and I did crazy things ... those things we do when we're young, but not anymore and. ... I lived in New York and Europe and I spent my time riding in trains, seeing the world, traveling on the tracks, taking photos, and I wanted to be a photographer and then one day ... I hardly remember it now. Well, I got married.

DANIEL: You got married!

VICTORIA: Yes, but —

DANIEL: In the church? *(Pause. He understands the answer is "yes.")* **I can't believe it!**

VICTORIA: It doesn't matter. It was kid stuff. ...

DANIEL: And you got married in the church again, with me!

VICTORIA: I didn't even remember that I had been married before!

DANIEL: Just a small lapse!

VICTORIA: I was. ...

DANIEL: A detail, a little thing, nothing important!

VICTORIA: It's just —

DANIEL: It just so happens that little things like, this ... that I married some Ramani and I did it in the church, those things slip your mind, of course! It's like a train station where you don't get off, right? No big deal. The name, who cares about the name? What a thing to forget! Honestly, Victoria. This I find hard to believe!!!

VICTORIA: You didn't believe.

DANIEL: And that made it all right!

VICTORIA: I figured that since you didn't believe it didn't hurt you.

DANIEL: Meaning, you did remember that you were married before. It wasn't that it slipped your mind. You thought about it and decided not to tell me.

VICTORIA: It was a few seconds, I thought about it for a few seconds and everything was already over and done and that was all so long ago and, God, my God, God has nothing to do with you ... right? That's what you've always said, that you don't —

DANIEL: You lied to everyone, the priest, your family, your *father* if he finds out he'll die all over again, and me. ... I'm ... I'm the biggest idiot. Because ... *(Pause. He looks at her in terror.)* And the divorce? *(Pause.)*

VICTORIA: The divorce?

DANIEL: When did you get divorced? *(He looks at her. More terror.)* You did get divorced, didn't you, Victoria? *(She drops her head.)* You never got divorced, Victoria! *(VICTORIA, defeated, is about to cry.)* For God's sake!!! *(DANIEL goes to the bar and pours himself a drink, downs it, then immediately pours another, and another, and another until he physically tires of drinking. He puts the glass down and calms himself, but looks dazed. VICTORIA gets up, decisively, and goes to speak to him but he interrupts her.)* Tell me the truth.

VICTORIA: The truth it is.

DANIEL: To anything I ask.

VICTORIA: Fine.

DANIEL: What's inside the present?

VICTORIA: What?

DANIEL: The present. Didn't you ever open it?

VICTORIA: I didn't have time. But I'd guess it's wine. He liked to give people wine. He thought it was a classy present. We were all dirt poor back then.

DANIEL: It says: "No hard feelings." Did you fight?
VICTORIA: We had split up that day.
DANIEL: The day you lost the bag?
VICTORIA: I was moving. We were getting separated. I put all my stuff into that bag and ran out. He stopped me and gave me the present. I didn't open it. I went to catch the subway. ...
DANIEL: Where you lost the bag. And him? Who was he? What kind of name is that ... Ramir?
VICTORIA: Ramani.
DANIEL: What kind of name is it, huh? *(VICTORIA goes and drinks what is left of DANIEL's last glass. Suddenly her hand trembles, visibly. She takes Georgia and squeezes her. She goes over to the bag. She sees the present, but DANIEL's shout breaks her concentration.)* **Answer me!**
VICTORIA: Okay. I'll tell you everything, at least what I remember. *(She sits beside him.)* Ramani was a guy I met in a bar. He was from Iran or Syria, I don't know. Saudi, I think.
DANIEL: You got married under Islam? *(She nods and he looks grim.)*
VICTORIA: We went out several times, we were a group of friends. After six months or so he said, "Let's get married" and like a fool I said yes. It didn't seem like a big deal at the time. We stayed together until little by little we grew apart. That day, when I lost my hand luggage, was the last day I saw him.
DANIEL: You never discussed a divorce?
VICTORIA: You may not believe it, but no. I left New York, I went to Europe, I traveled all over the world. I made my life, I started over. I became an anchorwoman and then I met you. I started over, my last life. My life with you. My home, what I am.
DANIEL: You've started a lot of lives.
VICTORIA: All I needed to meet you.
DANIEL: You sound like a cheap Valentine. Maybe that's what

you are.

VICTORIA: Daniel, you never talked to me like that.

DANIEL: I don't know what to do, Victoria. I feel like I'm on a plane in a nosedive. Like a doll. ... What do we have to do? If you never got divorced, our marriage is nullified. You've committed a crime and —

VICTORIA: We'll do whatever we need to. We'll do whatever you want. Whatever you think we should.

DANIEL: Is there anything else in that bag that could change my life?

VICTORIA: I don't think so.

DANIEL: How come you never told me any of this? How many secrets are you hiding? Are you crazy? Are you crazy Victoria? Are you crazy? Are you crazy? Are you crazy? Are you crazy? Are you crazy? Are you crazy? Are you crazy?

About Face
by Noëlle Janaczewska

1   Kilobyte — Male, teens
2   Daisy — Female, teens
3   Tarwater — Female, teens
4
5   *The following "scene" is really two scenes extracted from*
6   *this play that the author describes as a "choral script": the*
7   *drama interweaves two time frames throughout, and many of*
8   *the passages are sung. In these two scenes, the three young*
9   *people are recounting for the police what actually happened*
10   *one night when they were practicing their choir rehearsal in a*
11   *boarded-up building just before the storm struck. The two*
12   *scenes may be done separately, one as a man-woman scene*
13   *(Kilobyte and Daisy) and the other as a monolog; or both may*
14   *be presented as a single unit, with Tarwater listening to the*
15   *others and then giving her account after the other two have*
16   *left. The nonrealistic, elusive, and poetic dialog alternates with*
17   *responses to questions from the police officers. The language*
18   *provides a strong challenge for the choices that young actors*
19   *can make in speaking the rich imagery and the rhyme, and*
20   *capturing the rhythmic flow while strong emotions must*
21   *underpin their delivery. At some points in the text the actors*
22   *can also decide which character delivers which lines, or the*
23   *director may assign lines to each.*
24
25   **KILOBYTE and DAISY:** I've got a sister: Frankie-boy. She's the
26   favoured son. She's the chip off the old block and he's the
27   sawdust.
28   Once she slapped my cheek so crazy-hard it opened up
29   a warehouse inside my head.

His dad's always making speeches about a glorious return to the homeland.

Where no one's been allowed to die and nothing's changed.

Naturally.

I'd love to be clever – like Jonah or Tarwater – and turn my mamma and the rest of them into a multiculti comedy – but I can't. Can I Rosebud?

I suppose you've heard it nuts and bolts five times over.

Don't know that we've much to add. Thanks, white no sugar. And black and three for me.

Let's think. We were singing in that rat infested, bat infested building.

But you know that already. Me? I work the front office of my stepfather's concern. No, not for me thank you very much, I'm fat-free.

Her mum was a ballet dancer you see.

Trained in the tradition of pain and malnutrition.

Whereas for my papa local food is only ever a tasteless copy of the fabulous fruits of home.

No, nothing to speak of or springing to mind. Don't you agree Bubs? There were winds piling on other winds.

And then the sirens. When it was over, we looked about but she'd vanished into thin air. I wish we could tell you more – *(DAISY and KILOBYTE get up and leave.)*

But we can't.

Sorry.

TARWATER: What I was doing while all the trouble was brewing?
Singing my heart out and goose guts and tapioca same as everyone else.

Sure, I'd noticed the construction site. Shadows beside themselves. The two nightwatchmen, yawns like orchids, cursing the universe.

No, I'm not especially political. To be honest I get sick of ministers banging on about the bloody family. They should meet my dad. After all his marriage to the bottle has lasted nearly thirty years. A union consummated every evening without fail.

Just a minute. I need to clear the cobwebs and candle-ends from my brain. Okay, fire away.

That's correct. I've applied to finish my thesis in a foreign city. Long afternoons of unpronounceable streets.

Haphazard? Last I saw of her she was footing on a narrow edge. Then smoke clouds filled the space between us and flames came razoring over the scrub.

Back to the beginning — but I've told you the story, every damn hiccup and bristle. All right, all right, keep your hair on.

It was choir practice like any other.

There was a slight breeze. ...

Tagged
by Susan Battye

1 Ms. Gibbons — 20s–40s
2 Spike — Teens
3
4 *This amusing two-character scene is grounded upon two*
5 *typical school characters: Spike, the school rebel, and Ms.*
6 *Gibbons, the deputy principal, who are waiting outside the*
7 *principal's office. Spike spins on the floor, break dance style. Ms.*
8 *Gibbons stands guard with a file in her hand. The scene*
9 *contains clear and sharp development for each character so that*
10 *each is changed and in a different place at the end from where*
11 *they began. There are also plenty of opportunities for each*
12 *character to play discoveries, game-playing, and conflict — and*
13 *certainly abundant comedy — as the action unfolds.*
14
15 GIBBONS: Will you stop that, Spike? You're doing me head in.
16 SPIKE: Good floor for doing spins. Wasted in here.
17 GIBBONS: Draw attention to yourself, why don't you, outside
18   the Principal's office.
19 SPIKE: Ms. Gibbons, what do you suggest I do? Sit and bite me
20   nails? Don't think so.
21 GIBBONS: What are you going to say to Mr. Crispin?
22 SPIKE: Nothin'.
23 GIBBONS: Have you seen that room he puts you in if you don't
24   talk?
25 SPIKE: You mean the one with no windows?
26 GIBBONS: Yeah. You stay there all day.
27 SPIKE: Sweet. Don't have to go to class.
28 GIBBONS: No going to the caff at interval to see your friends.
29 SPIKE: Who cares? Sick of that crowd anyway.

GIBBONS: No getting out at lunch.
SPIKE: Ain't got no lunch.
GIBBONS: No music to plug into your brain.
SPIKE: Sensory deprivation! No!
GIBBONS: And we take your cell phone off you.
SPIKE: *(Shocked)* Now that's against the law. Cell phone's personal property. There's a lot of private information in there.
GIBBONS: Spike. We are the law.
SPIKE: That's what you think.
GIBBONS: The walls have ears, Spike.
SPIKE: What? Where?
GIBBONS: We saw you at the lockers.
SPIKE: What a load of crap!
GIBBONS: Think about it. How come you got picked up so fast?
SPIKE: The weasel on office duty told on me?
GIBBONS: Wrong. We tracked your cell phone.
SPIKE: Never! I've done nothing!
GIBBONS: "Bombing's da bomb!" Wasn't that the title of your little impromptu speech to the English class on Wednesday?
SPIKE: Mighta been.
GIBBONS: "A blow for freedom of speech," you said.
SPIKE: You can't pin this on me. Where's the evidence?
GIBBONS: Where you left it in fluorescent pink half an hour ago on the Principal's car.
SPIKE: Not me.
GIBBONS: "Creepy Crispin Eats Cockroaches." How is that "a blow for freedom of speech," pray tell?
SPIKE: The people gotta know the truth.
GIBBONS: What's that got to do with cockroaches, Spike?
SPIKE: Work it out for yourself, Ms. Gibbons.
GIBBONS: Your aim would be what? To go where no tagger's gone before?
SPIKE: My aim is to get out of this hole as fast as possible. Can I go now?

GIBBONS: Not until we've had a little chat. I want to know what goes on inside that head of yours, Spike, so that I can help you. Mr. Crispin is very upset about his car. Almost a thousand dollars worth of damage. And we all know it's not the first time.

SPIKE: That guy needs a personality transplant. No way people ever gonna listen to reason in this place.

GIBBONS: *(Warning)* Spike! So you hang off the bridges and climb on to parapets to get your "message" in our faces! Yeah?

SPIKE: True.

GIBBONS: Get your tag on every road sign, garage door that's shut to you all over town so that everyone pays you due respect, right?

SPIKE: Respect. That's what it's all about. R-E-S-P-E-C-T.

GIBBONS: Be like a shadow in the night and leave no trace behind. Isn't that your motto?

SPIKE: How would you know?

GIBBONS: You wrote it in red on the cover of the tattooing book you returned to the library this morning.

SPIKE: Double whammy.

GIBBONS: And then what happened?

SPIKE: You tell me.

GIBBONS: You bombed the Principal's car. ...

SPIKE: It needed a paint job.

GIBBONS: In the staff car park in broad daylight with a mini-cam watching your every move.

SPIKE: Wasn't there the day before.

GIBBONS: That's technology for you. There's no way you're going to get out of this one, Spike.

SPIKE: So?

GIBBONS: What's the worst that could happen?

SPIKE: I get locked in the white room for an hour with Creepy and his bad breath?

GIBBONS: Wrong. You get expelled.

SPIKE: More time to find new walls and parapets, eh, miss?

1 GIBBONS: Your mum and dad won't be impressed.
2 SPIKE: I'll be mincemeat. Why are you telling me this?
3 GIBBONS: We could do a deal here.
4 SPIKE: With the devil? No, thanks!
5 GIBBONS: Think of me as your spiritual advisor.
6 SPIKE: You what?
7 GIBBONS: I asked Mr. C. and he said I could be your "support
8   person."
9 SPIKE: What, like a crutch? *(Sniggers.)*
10 GIBBONS: On the level, Spike. We need your talents.
11 SPIKE: Come again?
12 GIBBONS: How does a year's free supply of spray paint sound
13   to you?
14 SPIKE: You're losing it, you are!
15 GIBBONS: Bridges, parapets, car park walls — they're all yours
16   for the taking.
17 SPIKE: How?
18 GIBBONS: Publicity for your alma mater.
19 SPIKE: You leave my mother out of this or I'll sue.
20 GIBBONS: No, Spike, alma mater, old school! For the school,
21   Spike, the *school*. Our numbers are down. You've got the
22   "X-factor." We want you to go out there and paint the town
23   red with our name. All undercover, of course.
24 SPIKE: Of course.
25 GIBBONS: Give us the "Cool School" image on every wall in town
26   and there'll be no more trouble and a clean promotion into
27   the next class — oh, and a little "help" with exams on the
28   side. Deal?
29 SPIKE: No white room?
30 GIBBONS: No white room.
31 SPIKE: No Creepy?
32 GIBBONS: No Creep ... er ... Mister Crispin to worry about.
33 SPIKE: Then it's a deal, Ms. Gibbons. *(Shaking hands:)* **Gotta**
34   **hand it to you, Ms. Gibbons, for a deputy principal, you're**
35   **an artist. A real artist.**

No Pain, No Gain
by Susan Battye

1. Young Man
2. Admissions Clerk

This hilarious scene moves swiftly from one gag to the next and shouldn't leave the audience time to think as the conversation quickly tangles and untangles itself. The structure is very clear and challenges the actors to pace themselves, using the dialog to discover the scene's rhythm. The confusion steadily mounts to reach a sharp climax of confusion in the last moments. The Admissions Clerk can be played by either a male or female.

YOUNG MAN: Owwww! *(The ADMISSIONS CLERK bounces up from behind the counter with file in hand.)*
CLERK: Good morning, good morning, good morning!
YOUNG MAN: Don't do that!
CLERK: How may I help you on this bright sunny day, sir?
YOUNG MAN: It's raining. Is this the – ?
CLERK: In here it's always sunny, sir. Now would you be ... ?
YOUNG MAN: What?
CLERK: You would be ... ?
YOUNG MAN: *(Waving his arm in the air)* Sore! Is this the –
CLERK: Right. Good. Mr. Sore, how can I help you?
YOUNG MAN: Come again?
CLERK: *(Pointing to the sign)* **Swifty Repair Services at your service, Mr. Sore. We are here for you, the customer, twenty-four/seven. Zero wait time is our goal. We're putting positivity before profits by making the most of people like you. It's awesome that you're coming on the**

team, batting for the right side, and we want you to know that you are a valued client.

YOUNG MAN: *(Annoyed)* I want to see your —

CLERK: Our client-based survey needs a little moment of your time, Mr. Sore. Did I mention the week in Hawaii under a coconut palm?

YOUNG MAN: No. Look, is this the —

CLERK: Do we have a deal for you! Sun-drenched beaches and a time-share condominium at your disposal. All transfers paid for, providing that you win, of course. The details required include your mother's dental records.

YOUNG MAN: Uhmmm ... I don't have that information.

CLERK: You don't? Well then, how do you repair her false teeth?

YOUNG MAN: They're no longer with us.

CLERK: So you've lost them? Oh, that's too bad!

YOUNG MAN: She's gone over to the other side.

CLERK: No! Surely not! Our football team is the best in the country. That's just not cricket!

YOUNG MAN: She's popped her clogs!

CLERK: We don't discriminate. Dutch, American, Chinese, Tahitian — it's all one world in here.

YOUNG MAN: *(Yelling)* She's presently deceased, I'm telling you!

CLERK: Deceased, eh? Obviously she didn't deal with Swifty Repairs. Never mind. Your mother could be embalmed by our Swifty Repairs Mortuary and transported to a Hawaiian island at no cost to yourself, of course, for a fun-filled weekend. No one will ever know you lost her false teeth.

YOUNG MAN: Ashes to ashes, dust to dust. No false teeth to repair. No forms to fill in! No trips to win. Geddit? My mother is gone, gone, gone!

CLERK: And sold! To the highest bidder! To the man in the pink shirt with the chest and the gold chains! Now I'm getting the picture. Was there a reason you came in?

YOUNG MAN: *(Waving the bandaged arm around)* **I am in pain!!!**

CLERK: Pain is our middle name. You want pain, you've come

to the right place. But we can fix it! Sign this form authorizing us to take lots of money out of your bank account. ...
YOUNG MAN: I've lost all my money.
CLERK: You need a bank.
YOUNG MAN: I've been to a bank. And then I cut myself.
CLERK: Shaving?
YOUNG MAN: What?
CLERK: Were you shaving?
YOUNG MAN: What do *you* think?
CLERK: I think you want me to examine you.
YOUNG MAN: You're right.
CLERK: What language?
YOUNG MAN: Pardon?
CLERK: What language would you like me to examine you in?
YOUNG MAN: What have you got?
CLERK: Swahili, Urdu, Persian, Italian, Maori, Chinese, Latin. ...
YOUNG MAN: English?
CLERK: On special. Half-price.
YOUNG MAN: Great.
CLERK: Can you sign this form in triplicate?
YOUNG MAN: What is it?
CLERK: It's a mere formality in case you die under the knife.
YOUNG MAN: Knife? What knife?
CLERK: First time, is it?
YOUNG MAN: What are you planning to do?
CLERK: No need to worry. Our work is guaranteed to please and you'll be all better before we can say "knife" — oops!
YOUNG MAN: Look, can I please see someone who's qualified around here?
CLERK: Qualified? Qualified? I am qualified. Read this. *(Turns the "Admissions" sign around.)* **Read!**
YOUNG MAN: *(Reading)* B.A., Ph.D., L.L.B., what's all this?
CLERK: Now the other eye.
YOUNG MAN: What?

CLERK: Try reading with the other eye.

YOUNG MAN: What for?

CLERK: *(Patiently)* To see if you have twenty-twenty vision, of course!

YOUNG MAN: There's nothing wrong with my eyes. Look, can I please see —

CLERK: You want to see someone qualified. I am qualified *(Points to the sign.)* ... over-qualified for this job. *(Points to the L.L.B.)* My last job I was prosecuting people who look a bit like you.

YOUNG MAN: I beg your pardon!

CLERK: Granted. The one before that I was researching the frustration people experience standing in line.

YOUNG MAN: That's me!

CLERK: No, it's not. I'd remember someone like you.

YOUNG MAN: What do I have to do to get admitted around here?

CLERK: Be dead, dying or on fire. Which is it to be?

YOUNG MAN: Dead. *(He falls dead in front of the counter.)*

CLERK: *(Calling)* Hey Sampson, got another one for the morgue! That's the tenth today dropped dead at the counter! Whadya know? Sure keeps the wait time down! *(Bangs a bell on the counter.)* **Next!**

Extended Monologs for Men

"On Guard"
by Marilyn Rofsky
from *She of the Lovely Ankle* by Women At Play

Bruce — Indeterminate age   Comic

 This is an exciting and unusual piece for a versatile actor capable of playing three roles simultaneously (with maybe a little hint of ventriloquism thrown in!). Bruce is a three-headed dog, the mythical creature named Cerberus who guarded the gates of Hades. The monolog is built around the characters of the god Hades, his fierce watchdog Cerberus, and the beautiful mortal Persephone, who has inflamed Hades' passion. The actor has a dog's head atop his own head, and another dog's head in each hand. (The piece is hilarious with the actor talking just to his hands!) The lines for each head are designated Bruce 1, Bruce 2, Bruce 3. In addition to the comic interplay between the three "heads," the piece also offers the actor a good problem-solving struggle and a clear character change and development from the start to the finish. In the original production, the setting was the entrance to a corporation's lower basement, suggested by a stool, with a table nearby, on which was a Styrofoam cup of coffee and a telephone.

BRUCE 1: *(Speaking to the audience, taking them into his confidence)* **Watch, he says. Watch! Remain at the entrance and watch for her. Me! Head of security for a multi-million dollar corporation relegated to the role of night watchman.**
BRUCE 2: Come on, be honest. You're not head of security for the corporation, just for this hell hole, this lower basement.
BRUCE 1: Okay, okay, so I guard the lower basement. So, that's an important job, isn't it? I can't let anybody out. I can't let

anybody in. That takes all three of us to accomplish, and now he wants me to waste my time lying in wait for one innocent female and then rush like an overeager law enforcement trainee to tell him that she has finally come his way, descended to our level. I won't do it. I'll refuse and demand to see — in black and white — where it says in my job description that I must immediately report the arrival of Persephone, so a certain male executive in the firm can lure her into his office for "late night business," as he put it with that smarmy style of his. I'm going to report Hayden's ridiculous command to my union representative. *(He picks up the phone and begins to dial.)*

BRUCE 3: But, wait. How do I know the union leaders won't view this as a frivolous call, a petty complaint by a worker merely looking out for himself, not for his fellow union members? They might hold it against me when the time comes for elections or negotiations.

BRUCE 1: You're right. I won't call. I don't want to jeopardize my career. *(He hangs up the phone.)*

BRUCE 2: I know what I'll do. I'll turn my eyes on him, Mister Executive Testosterone Himself. I'll watch him closely as he spends hours in his office devising ways to lure that poor girl here instead of working on making everyone else here accountable as he's supposed to do. I'll keep track of his every memo, his every phone call, his every move not directly related to business, but to his passion, his Persephone.

BRUCE 3: But wait. That could backfire. Employees might misconstrue my plan to unnerve him as a loss of trust in his managerial abilities. I might unwittingly instill paranoia, fear and panic so that worker productivity plummets along with profits. No, I refuse to be responsible for financial disaster.

BRUCE 1: So ... here I am again ... watching ... yet, not quite. I mean, there's watching and then there's really watching. I can intimidate when I *really* watch. It's a gift, actually. "Eyes in the back of his heads," my mother used to say. But I'll watch casually, not putting my heart into my work, sipping a cup of coffee. *(He picks up the Styrofoam coffee cup from the table and sips.)* **Real coffee, of course, to which I am entitled, not this day-old, over-perked, reheated decaf stuff in this regulation six-ounce Styrofoam cup from the lunch room. And it won't be that vending machine, pseudo-Colombian bean substance labeled "regular-light." I'll drink a deep, dark brew from a personalized mug and then, only occasionally watch for the woman of the hour.**

BRUCE 2: Right you are. I'm refusing to *truly* watch as told; I'm only watching *my* way.

BRUCE 3: Hold on a minute. That won't work. Everyone will view me as some lazy, overpaid-for-little work, possible family member of the big boss — who else would dare to sit and sip coffee on company time, they'll all ask, not knowing that I am Head of Security. I won't lower myself to become that kind of watchman.

BRUCE 1: Head of Security. Well, hell, security for what may be the most important area in the whole operation, depending on which way you look at it. I refuse to have my dignity, my training, my expertise trashed by less than full watching. I'll stand up right now. I'll dazzle the visitors, temp secretaries, and dignitaries with my keenness of eyes and investigative powers. I never refuse a challenge. If Persephone dares to descend, and Sam actually lets her out of the elevator, I'll lead her right into the lion's den. I'll assume the best damned watchman stance this firm has ever seen. *(He puts the coffee cup down and assumes a pose.)*

"Sam"
by Katherine Burkman
from *She of the Lovely Ankle* by Women At Play

Sam — Indeterminate age　　　　　　　　　　　　　　　Comic

This unusual piece can be performed with or without a female "listening" and reacting in the role of Persephone, but it's certainly best done as a two-character piece with a non-speaking actress onstage. The situation is a modern adaptation of the story of Persephone, the Greek myth about the abduction of Persephone by Hades, lord of the underworld. Here the setting is instead a corporate headquarters where an elevator — run by the indecisive Sam, who is a modern version of Sisyphus, takes souls up and down from the sub-basement. In this section of the play, Persephone has been trying to persuade Sam to let her descend to the sub-basement where the "tortured" souls of the dead are kept. (Ironically, in this modern version Persephone asks to visit the underworld.) The monolog permits the actor to play a powerful struggle from beginning to end; it also challenges the actor to structure his character development clearly so that Sam can completely reverse himself by the time the piece concludes.

SAM: I'm going down, Persephone, because I have to before I go up, and I have to go up before I go down. That's what I do. Up, then down. But I can't let you out in the lower basement, and you know it. I've told you year in and year out, it's against the rules. Against the rules. *(PERSEPHONE stamps her foot.)* I know, I know, I'm here because I broke the rules. But there's a lot more they can do to me, Persephone. You're such an innocent. Anyhow, why go down? You belong amidst a field of flowers, not a cavern of rubies. *(PERSEPHONE puts her hands on her hips in fury.)* You don't have to worry about those people in the lower basement. Those rumors about their condition are unfounded. They are not lost, purposeless, and dehydrated, nor do I think your art work would cheer them up. And dear girl, what would your mother say? I'm much more scared of her than I am of your uncle. She'd bury me alive. *(PERSEPHONE makes silent laughter.)* You're right. I have to admit that I feel buried alive every time I make the elevator go up. That's when my tendency to claustrophobia takes over. But the descents are quite different, my dear. It may be hard for you to understand at your age, but as I return to the bottom, only to begin again, my mind is strangely free, confined though I may be. See? I'm even a poet. *(Pause. PERSEPHONE pulls at his sleeve.)* **I can't open the door here,** Persephone. Once you get off, there's no going back. You're young, beautiful, fresh, fragrant, fleshy, fanciful, forward-looking. None of that applies below. It would be a terrible waste. *(PERSEPHONE sits down on the floor, crosses her arms, adamant that she won't move.)* And think of your mom. I remember the wonders she works. If I could start over again, I wouldn't go to business school. I'd just shadow your mother. She's the one with the secrets. If she weren't keeping her eye on that CEO and his Board, there'd be total blight. Demi loves you, Persephone – she's just busy. *(PERSEPHONE gets down on the floor of the elevator, puts her ear to the floor.)* They are not calling you. You're just having bad dreams and you think it's them, calling to you. And anyway, you'd never get past Bruce. He always keeps one head facing the elevator. *(PERSEPHONE takes a piece of cake out of her purse and moves SAM over. She takes the imaginary elevator controls.)* If you took over for me, what makes you think I'd come back? I ran away before. I was given three days to see to my affairs and come back. Did I return? No. I had no wish to be buried alive. I didn't show. **Well, they got me. That's why I'm here.** *(PERSEPHONE kisses SAM on the cheek. He moves her away from the elevator controls.)* **It's a terrible risk. For both of us. Okay, Persephone. Remember, I'll be here, waiting for the greatest coffee break in time. Lower basement. All out.** *(He opens the door and PERSEPHONE exits.)*

bobrauschenbergamerica
by Charles L. Mee

Bob — Indeterminate age   Serious

    This extended monolog takes the form of a murderer attempting to justify his act and win forgiveness from his listener. It is best played with a vis-à-vis located in the audience — "the public." The actor should structure the piece carefully in order to avoid presenting a rambling and unfocussed discourse. From the beginning, Bob desperately craves forgiveness; this is why he must speak. And the piece does reach a climax in the last section, where we finally understand what Bob wants of us. This presents the actor with a strong challenge.

BOB: And yet, I think, nonetheless,
     forgiveness is possible. ...

     Well, sure,
     Really under any circumstances.

     Uh, primarily, uh, uh, the, uh, the ...
     primarily the question is
     does man have the power to forgive himself.
     And he does.
     That's essentially it.
     I mean if you forgive yourself,
     and you absolve yourself of all, uh,
     of all wrongdoing in an incident,
     then you're forgiven.
     Who cares what other people think, because uh. ...

Not until I was reading the Aquarian Gospel did I,
did I strike upon,
you know I had almost had ends meet because I had certain
uh, you know,
to-be-or-not-to-be reflections about, of course, what I did.
And uh. ...

Triple murder.
Sister, husband. Sister, husband
and a nephew, my nephew.
And uh, uh, you know, uh, manic depressive. ...

It was a knife.
It was a knife. ...

Yes. ...

Sssssss ... *(Points to slitting his throat.)*
like that. ...

It has already become part of my past. ...

In the first three or four years there was a couple of nights where I would stay up thinking about how I did it, you know. And what they said ... they told me later there were something like thirty stab wounds in my sister, but uh, I remember distinctly I just cut her throat once. ... That was all, you know, and I don't know where the thirty stab wounds came from. So that might have been some kind of blackout thing. You know, I was trying to re- re- uh, re-uh, uh, resurrect the uh, the crime – my initial steps, etcetera. You know, and uh, and uh, I took, as a matter of fact, it came right out of the, was staring at the New Testament at the time, as a matter of fact, I'm about the only person you'll ever meet that went to, to do a triple murder with a Bible in his, is his pocket, and, and, listening to a radio. I had delusions of grandeur with the radio. Uh, I had a red shirt on that was symbolic of, of some lines in Revelation in the, in the New Testament. Uh, I had a red motor ... as a matter of fact, I think it was chapter six something, verses three, four or five, or something where, uh it was a man, it was a man. On a red horse. And, and, a man on a red horse came out, and uh, and uh, uh, he was given a knife, and unto him was given the power to kill and destroy. And I actually thought I was this person. And I thought that my red horse was this red Harley Davidson I had. And I wore ... it was just, you know, it was kind of a symbolic type of thing. And, and, and uh, you know, uh, after the murders I thought the nephew was, was the, was a new devil or something, you know. This, this is pretty bizarre now that I think back on it. I thought he was a new devil and uh, uh. I mean basically I love my sister, there's no question about that. But at times my sister hadn't come through, uh, for me. You know and I was in another one of these manic attacks. And uh, and uh, uh, uh, you know, uh, I was just uh, I was just you know, I mean I was fed up with all this, you know, one day they treat me good and then they tell all these other people that I was a maniac and watch out for me and etcetera and like that. And uh, uh, so I went to them that night to tell them I was all in trouble again, you know, and could they put me up for the night, you know, and they told me to take a hike and uh, so uh, believing that I had the power to kill, uh, you know, that was that for them. You know. I mean when family turns you out, that's a real blow. You know. But uh, back to the original subject of forgiveness. If I forgive myself, I'm forgiven. You know that's essentially the answer. I'm the captain of my own ship. I run my own ship. Nobody can crawl in my ship unless they get permission. I just *(He nods.)* "over there." You know. "I'm forgiven." You know. Ha-ha. You know. *(Laughs.)* It's as simple as that. You know. You're your own priest, you're your own leader, you're your own captain. You know. You run your own show, a lot of people know that.

Extended Monologs for Women

Saints and Angels
by Shirley King

Joanie — Teens　　　　　　　　　　　　　　　　Seriocomic

This amusing monolog "updates" the character of Joan of Arc to the contemporary world, where the playwright poses questions about how the historical heroine might respond to the problems and issues we face today. It offers a rich challenge to the actor, who will find pain, longing, humor, surprise, and discovery in the palette of Joanie's emotions. However, the actor must avoid performing the piece in a rambling, impulsive, and unstructured manner, because there is also a strong subtext of love running beneath the spoken text that drives the presentation forward and finally emerges only at the conclusion.

JOANIE: I was a model child. Obedient to my parents, industrious, unselfish and kind to the neighbors. I also excelled in the domestic arts, spinning and sewing. But well, you know how teenagers get. I began hearing voices. Saint Michael, Saint Catherine, Saint Margaret.

They didn't just say, "Be a good girl, Jeanette," for that was my name at the time. They said, "Go drive the English from our land." Well, how many girls get an opportunity like that? I had to go — carrying my own banner of painted lilies with an angel on each side.

While leading the Dauphin's army, I freed Orleans. Oh, but that's just the beginning. I also helped Charles become King, crowned in the cathedral of Rheims.

But then you know how kings are. Fickle. Yes. And ungrateful. Charles grew disenchanted with me so I left the Court. I went on killing English soldiers but to tell the truth my heart wasn't in it.

I was captured at Compiègne on May 23rd, 1430 — condemned as a witch and a heretic — is it a heretic or an heretic? I'm never quite sure.

They had a large bonfire, and I assume you know the rest. But here's the best part: those earlier findings of heresy were overturned! In 1920 the Church of Rome officially declared me a saint. Yes. A Saint. You may wish to take note of this: my personal feast day is celebrated May 30th.

(JOANIE removes her Joan of Arc costume as she speaks. She is dressed in jeans, a T-shirt and running shoes. She carries a backpack.)

I returned in 1963, a newborn infant, sent back to make a difference. But now I am married to a man named Sam who does not believe in me. He believes in God, in whom he has infinite faith, but not in me.

But you see, I have an option. Kill him? Oh no. Not this century. I am so over that. I simply need to make a new life for myself. So — I decided to go to Afghanistan.

I first met Afrah while asking directions. "Be careful if you go into the country," she said. "There are land mines." Afrah lost her left leg to a blast mine made in Iraq or Russia.

Afrah means Happiness. Her sister was called Huma. Huma is a bird living in a quiet area. When a Huma bird flies to the city it fills the people with joy. Huma — the woman, not the bird — was killed by Al Qaeda. Accidentally, Afrah assumes, because intentions are so important.

You wonder what I carry in this backpack? *(She shows several items as she speaks.)* **Jeans, T-shirts, towels, books, soap, shampoo, duct tape, a Walkman, Nyquil, granola bars and the Holy Bible. Survival gear.**

How did I get to Kabul? Oh, that's a story in itself. I flew to Pakistan and hired a car. We drove on rutted roads at thirty miles an hour through dust storms. Sixteen hours on the road and my driver dumped me as soon as he could. Pakistan was his home and he felt safer there. Can you imagine anyone now feeling safe anywhere?

I was looking for a hospital, with good reason.

You see, I'm awfully good at giving injections and changing bandages – skills my sister Lulu taught me. She's a nurse.

Lulu thinks I am insane for coming here. Nothing new. Some called me insane for obeying those terrifying commands from Saint Michael, Saint Catherine, and Saint Margaret. Perhaps I shouldn't have listened. But I was only seventeen.

These days their advice is more benign. I should love my neighbor, make peace not war, lend a helping hand *(Pause.)* Well, I never said the saints were original. But I congratulate them for finally knowing that war is evil.

I was looking for a children's hospital, I told Afrah. Could she direct me?

"Things are better now," she said. "The British help with medicine, running water and supplies." She agreed to take me there.

I didn't want to trouble her. But Afrah insisted. She showed me her artifical leg, which they gave her at Karte-Seh. "You may wish to cover your head," she said. "You will feel safer if you do."

Oh. Well ... I would have to get back to her on that. And of course, I was sorry about her sister.

As we walked the dusty road single file, Afrah said she was trying to understand our country. "First you support the Taliban, then you kill them. Now you come to help us. We need your help, so we are grateful. Grateful but confused. Follow me. Less than half a mile now."

In the hospital I met Doctor Henry Maxwell from San Francisco.

Before saying hello he demanded to know if I had a gun in my knapsack. A gun? Really! A gun. It seems that Doctor Maxwell did not want anyone shooting up the place — accidentally or otherwise.

No guns, no swords, I told him.

But why was this man so disagreeable? Did I look like a terrorist? I came to help, not to harm.

"Forgive me," he said, "but have you ever seen kids whose legs were blown off by land mines? Pretty horrendous."

I'm good at giving shots and bathing patients. Will that do or should I go to medical school first? Snippy? Yes. Well, I was exhausted. But then Doctor Maxwell explained that some people came to be of service and could not be. It was all too much. "Are you one of those?" he asked, as he had every right. Still, I resented the question.

In this life I was eager to help women and children. Couldn't he tell? Social reforms were not in place — this I understood — but would surely come in time.

Obviously being burned at the stake had not cured me of naïveté.

What I now know is that banishing Al Qaeda hasn't reformed anything. Women in Afghanistan are still beaten and sent to prison for nothing more than leaving their husbands.

On my very first day, Doctor Maxwell invited me to take the tour. I would be horrified, he said, but should try not to act like it.

Children with stumps for arms and legs were in the first ward. I didn't react. "Good for you," he said. "Well, let's move on. Thirty minutes from now, let me know if you still want to be here."

Six months have passed. I'm still here, earning the

right to be called a saint. I haven't made it yet. Will I? Come back in six years and I'll let you know.

May I tell you what I do know? I know that the angel called Henry Maxwell has chronic colitis and screams in his sleep. But here in this hospital he is the King of Courage.

I also know this: I love Doctor Maxwell, far more than I ever loved King Charles.

Audition
by Cary Pepper

Raleigh — 20s   Comic

Raleigh is a clever young actress presenting herself at an audition for Sam and Jake, two producers who are seated in the house but are unseen.

RALEIGH: Your ad said you wanted to see a monologue. Are you looking for any particular kind of material? *(In response to SAM.)* **Something that shows range. ... All right ... I'd like to do something from "Romeo and Juliet."** *(She closes her eyes, takes a breath, goes into character, and begins.)* **O Romeo, Romeo, wherefore art thou Romeo? Deny thy father and refuse thy name, Or, if thou wilt not, be but sworn my love, And I'll no longer be a Capulet. 'Tis but thy name that is my enemy. Though art yourself ...** *(Corrects herself:)* **... th**y**self ... though no ...** *(Corrects herself:)* **... *not* a Montague. What's a Montague? It is not food, nor hand ...** *(Corrects herself:)* **... It is *nor hand,* nor *foot!* Nor arm, nor face belonging to a man. O, be some other man ...** *(Corrects herself:)* **.... Be some other *name!!*** *(Breaking character:)* **Look ... I've messed this up. Do you mind if I start over? I know, it's not professional to stop in the middle. Once you start something, you keep going, no matter what happens. And if it goes badly, turn it around, or use it. ... I've been taught all that. But that's a lot of classroom theory, and when you're out here ... *doing* it ... everything's different. And I realize that I've probably already blown it. Just by stopping and asking to do it over, I've completely messed this up. But that was *so bad.* So**

horribly inadequate. I won't be able to live with myself if I don't just stop right now and start over. I don't know what happened. ... *I know* this material. ... I know this *character.* Sometimes I think I am her! I mean, think about it. ... The thing she wants more than anything in the world. ... The man she loves with all her heart and soul ... is the *one* person she can't have. ... *That just rips your core out!!* Sometimes I lie awake at night and think about what that would be like! I think about how I'd bring this creature to life. ... But there, too, that's theory. And you can learn all the theory in the world, but when you're *here* ... everything changes. Every audition you go to. ... You wonder ... about *everything.* Who are these people? What are they like? What are they gonna say they're looking for? What are they *really* looking for? What are they thinking about you? What are they thinking that they're *not* saying? And ... what if ... what if ... you're not as good as you think you are? What if you'll *never* be as good as you hope to be? What if. ... What if you don't have any talent at all? What if you're just deluding yourself? Because there are plenty of people who *don't* have talent. But there are people who *do.* But there are lot of people with talent who never make it. But there are people who do make it. Which means *you* can, too. So you keep at it. Because it's what you want, more than anything in the world. And I walk in here and fool you into thinking I'm confident, when I ... am ... *terrified!* And I march to the edge of a precipice, and stand there, staring into the bottomless void ... and then ... I jump. You don't know ... you don't know the terror ... the heart-rending, back-breaking terror. ... You're putting it all on the line. ... Baring your soul ... and there ... is ... no ... place ... to ... hide. *I must be crazy!!!* I don't know how much longer I can keep doing this. But how can I stop? Give up the thing I want most in life? Because if I quit today. ... How will I get through tomorrow? So you keep going. ... Defeat after defeat, rejection after rejection. ... You go in and take another shot. And that's what I'm asking for now. Please ... please, can I start over? *(In response to SAM:)* Maybe I'm not cut out for this business? *(In response to JAKE:)* Not tough enough. ... You know how easy that is? For you to sit there and say that? You snap your fingers and we come running. ... "Okay, honey, you got something for us?" And *we* know, right off the bat, we're dealing with someone *else* who doesn't really care. Who, as soon as we stop, it's, "Okay, we've got your number, we know where to reach you." And three seconds after we walk out, it's "Next!" But you never see what goes on, on the other side of that door. You never see us when we sit alone at night, analyzing what we did wrong. And even what we did *right!* *(To SAM:)* Who the *hell* do you think you are! And don't give me that, "Aw, gee, what did I do?" look! You think *you* could do it? Hey, I asked you a question! *(Wheels on JAKE:)* Shut up! You have nothing to say to me! You don't have a *clue* what I'm talking about! But let me tell you something ... you should check people for weapons when they come in here. ... Because one of these days someone is gonna snap. Right before your predatory eyes and your, "What did I do?" faces. I could do it ... right now. ... Right now, I am inches ... seconds ... *nano*seconds from ripping your hearts out! And the only thing that's saving you ... both of you ... is ... *I want this part!* *(She catches herself.)* Oh no, I'm sorry ... I'm so sorry ... I don't know what came over me. When I walked in, all I wanted was a part in a play ... a few minutes after that, all I wanted was to start my monologue over. ... Now ... look what I've done. ... I don't know what to say ... what to do. ... How do you take it all back? How do I make it better? I'm losing it. ... I don't know what's going to happen next. ... I don't even know what I *want* to happen next. ... Yes, I do ... I know exactly what I want to happen. I want to stop time

and wind back the clock and make it all like it was before. But you can't. And now. ... Now ... I don't know what's happening to me!!! *(She sinks to the floor and buries her head in her hands and sobs. After awhile she slowly looks up, completely calm, and smiles.)* **So, was that enough range for you? Or would you like to see something else?**

Terrestrial and Without Imagination
by Luiza Carol

Dark Lady — 20s-30s   Seriocomic

This monolog doesn't have to be memorized since the actress is required to read it. These are ten imaginary letters to Shakespeare written by the "Dark Lady". The setting might be very simple, suggesting Shakespeare's period. Slight changes of setting and light should indicate that the letters are written on ten different days and at different hours. The Dark Lady should write and make pauses after each, or she may begin by putting the "final dot" and then read the whole letter. Perhaps two or three or more may be read by an actor playing Shakespeare, just receiving the letter and reading it. Or perhaps another actor might read some of Shakespeare's sonnets as letters that answer and/or trigger the Dark Lady's response.

                              1

DARK LADY: I am the lady of thy sonnets, or at least thou makest me think I am the one – although I'll never know how many more dark ladies thou makest think the same, for fun. Yes, I have left thee for a mutual friend. ... We wanted to escape thy haunting spell. ... A lie from the beginning to the end was all thy magical poetic hell. I need no verses facing space and time, nor lofty symbols of the human love, nor deepest wisdom molded into rhyme, nor mystic music from the realms above. Fidelity I need and can't forgive that 'tis the only thing thou canst not give.

2

A sermon about marriage – that is not the kind of answer thou art waiting for. Inside thy world of poetry so hot, the oaths are not respected any more. 'Tis always poetry that thou dost praise, while I prefer its substance: mine own home, the kitchen and the kindled fireplace, the cradle waiting for babes of mine own. I praise engagement rings – thou lookst upon such things as handcuffs for a slave; I need a faithful husband to climb the hill of age, both beautiful and brave. Fidelity I need and can't forgive that 'tis the only thing thou canst not give.

3

I loved the poet not the poetry; I craved for all his everlasting love. I wanted marriage and maternity; I craved for peaceful life, blessed from above. I can't create song lyrics in the moon, I don't write poems – I live inside one. 'Tis babes I can create inside my womb and in my kitchen there are soups I've done. Terrestrial and without imagination is mine own love, and never very far. I do not need exalted admiration, I know I'm not a diva or a star. Fidelity I need and can't forgive that 'tis the only thing thou canst not give.

4

I don't write metaphors, I'm not a poet. I write the words the way they come to me. I'm just a dark lady for thee – I know it; in songs and wine thou keepst forgetting me. I know that thou enjoyst my jealousy and like an actor thou dost trigger it, I know I'm not the only muse for thee and when I cry thou dost not care a bit. That's why I left thee, trying to destroy thy paper love tormenting like a curse. I long to have my children and enjoy my life, without the bitter taste of verse. Fidelity I need and can't forgive that 'tis the only thing thou canst not give.

5

I've never been torn between pan and pen – between the kitchen and the poetry. I took for granted that the two of them were making only one whole thing for me. I can't materialize the most divine of love in anything but pickles. Seems to me that my deep feelings most sublime become rich salads, puddings, cakes or creams. I don't crave for originality, I only try to do some useful cooking with no display of creativity; 'tis not for eulogies that I am looking. Fidelity I need and can't forgive that 'tis the only thing thou canst not give.

6

And if today I take in hand the quill and write to my forsaken lover, 'tis because a secret urge, unbridled, still runs in my heart. I lose control on this. Myself I cannot truly understand. ... The sonnet makes me lose my memory. ... What right hand writes—erases the left hand. ... Thou art the poet – I'm the poetry. Is it thy voice that lives deep inside me, or 'tis myself inside thy voice alive? Dost thou ache me, or my wound is in thee? I can't forgive and get thee off my life. Fidelity I need and can't forgive that 'tis the only thing thou canst not give.

7

I think in prose and yet I speak in rhymes. What happens to me is a thought transplant: I dream a strange graft grows in me sometimes. ... I'd tear it out ... but I wake up and can't. ... The alien dream in stinging hot tears hurts. ... I threw thy book in the fire yesterday, but 'tis in vain because thy magic words come back alive in my mind anyway – their frost and fire I can no longer fight. I throw myself to someone else's chest: he doesn't give me all the stars or night, but he will be a husband good and blessed. Fidelity I need and can't forgive that 'tis the only thing thou canst not give.

8

Oh no, I'm not sorry for what it was, not sorry for what couldn't have been. Yes, our love was truly meaningful, because it was the right step toward happiness. Had not it been, I wouldn't have known pain: could not appreciate the steadiness of a new lover and could never gain the blessings of my present happiness. Had not it been, I would have still longed for something so vague, so nameless that somehow my mind be never able to explore. ... But I am glad I know what I need, now: Fidelity I need and can't forgive that 'tis the only thing thou canst not give.

9

The man I love is sleeping by my side; he whispers thy name starting in his dreams. It is the same abyss in which we slide, it is the same love haunting our veins. There is no awful secret between us: we've learned to give and get exactly what we have in our souls – obtaining thus no more ... but yet no less. Though we have not forgotten thee, we don't try to forget the past. We know 'tis not forgetfulness, but deep serenity we need to get to achieve peace of mind and quietness. Fidelity we need and can't forgive that 'tis the only thing thou canst not give.

10

We both left thee, but didn't betray thee. Only to half of thee we said good-bye: we kept the Will of pure poetry and left the Will made up of filthy lie. Thou art a rotten lie of flesh and blood, our souvenirs of love are mere lies; only thy books are true, unsoiled by mud – we read from them in evenings with clear skies. And time is flowing back, erasing all that once was our only truth of life. Didst thou exist? Wast thou a leaf of fall, a dreamy fume, a dreamy sound of fife? Fidelity we need and shall have got, while cherishing thy poetry a lot.

Credits

About Face by Noëlle Janaczewska. Copyright © 2003 by Noëlle Janaczewska. All rights reserved. Production rights, in whole or part, by any group, amateur or professional, are retained by the author. Inquiries regarding production rights should be addressed to the author's agent at The Cameron Creswell Agency, 7th Floor, Marlborough Street, Surry Hills NSW 2010, (Sydney) Australia. Phone: +61 2 9319 7199; FAX: +61 2 9319 6866; Email: info@cameronsmanagement.com.au. *About Face* was commissioned by Powerhouse Youth Theatre and first produced by them in association with the School of Contemporary Arts, University of Western Sydney. It opened at Parramatta Riverside Theatres, Sydney, on 15 June 2002.

Another Way Out by Max Bush. Copyright © 2004 by Max Bush, is reprinted here by special arrangement of the author. All questions regarding performance royalties should be directed to Max Bush, 5372 132nd Avenue, Hamilton, Michigan 49419. Email: Maxb@egl.net

Audition by Cary Pepper. Copyright © 2003 by Cary Pepper. All rights reserved. Reprinted by permission. Information concerning rights should be addressed by email to the author: CaryPepper@aol.com

"Blind Date" by Ann Roth, from *The Blueberry Café,* by Women At Play. Copyright © 2003 by Woman At Play. All rights reserved. Reprinted by permission of the author. Inquiries regarding rights should be addressed to Katherine H. Burkman at 2990 Shadywood Rd., Columbus, OH 43221.

Blue Girl by Deborah Aita. Copyright © 2001 by Deborah Aita. All rights reserved. Production rights, in whole or part, by any group, amateur or professional, are retained by the author. Inquiries regarding production rights should be addressed to the author: Crow's Nest, 2 Crow Arch Lane, Crow, Ringwood, Hampshire BH24 1NZ UNITED KINGDOM. Email: debaita@freeuk.com

bobrauschenbergamerica by Charles L. Mee. Copyright © 2004 by Charles L. Mee. All rights reserved. Reprinted by permission. Information concerning rights should be addressed to the author's agent: Sam Cohn, ICM Inc., 40 W. 57th St., New York, NY 10019. Phone: (212) 556-5600.

Can't Believe It by R.N. Sandberg. Copyright ©2004 by R.N. Sandberg. All rights reserved. Reprinted by permission. Information concerning rights should be addressed to the author: R.N. Sandberg, 160 Bertrand Dr., Princeton, NJ 08540. Email: rsand@princeton.edu

"Competition" by Elizabeth Nash, from *It's Academic*, by Woman At Play. Copyright © 2001 by Women At Play. All rights reserved. Reprinted by permission of the author. Inquiries regarding rights should be addressed to Katherine H. Burkman at 2990 Shadywood Rd., Columbus, OH 43221.

"Distended Ear Lobes" by Katherine Burkman, from *She of the Lovely Ankle*, by Women At Play. Copyright © 2000 by Women At Play. All rights reserved. Reprinted by permission of the author. Inquiries regarding rights should be addressed to Katherine H. Burkman at 2990 Shadywood Rd., Columbus, OH 43221.

Fair(l)y (S)tale by Amanda Kellock. Copyright © 2003 by Amanda Kellock. All rights reserved. Reprinted by permission. Information concerning rights should be addressed to the author: 520 Church, Beaconsfield QC, H9W 3T1, Canada.

Guides by Josh Overton. Copyright © 2004 by Josh Overton. All rights reserved. Reprinted by permission. Information concerning rights should be addressed to the author: Josh@avenuecable.com.

Halls of Horror by Josh Overton. Copyright © 2004 by Josh Overton. All rights reserved. Reprinted by permission. Information concerning rights should be addressed to the author: Josh@avenuecable.com.

How His Bride Came to Abraham by Karen Sunde. Copyright © 1992 by Karen Sunde. All rights reserved. This work is fully protected under the copyright laws of the United States of America. No part of this publication may be photocopied, reproduced, stored in a retrieval system, or transmitted, in any form or by any means, electronic, mechanical, recording, or otherwise, without the prior permission of the publisher. Written permission is required for live performance of any sort. This includes readings, cuttings, scenes and excerpts. For amateur and stock performances, please contact Broadway Play Publishing, Inc., 56 E. 81st St., New York, NY 10028-0202. Phone: (212) 772-8334. FAX: (212) 772-8358. Website: www.broadwayplaypubl.com. For all other rights please contact the author at www.karensunde.com or ksunde@thorn.net

I'd Know You Anywhere by Dori Appel. Copyright © 1994 by Dori Appel. All rights reserved. Reprinted by permission. Production rights in whole or part, by any group, amateur or professional, are retained by the author. Inquiries regarding production rights should be addressed to the author at P.O. Box 1364, Ashland, OR 97520. Email: applcart@mind.net. Or contact her through www.geocities.com/doriappel

In the Laundromat by William Borden. Copyright © 2004 by William Borden. All rights reserved. No performance or reading of this work may be given without express permission of the author. Inquiries regarding rights should be addressed to the author at 7996 S. FM 548, Royse City, TX 75189. Email: wborden@paulbunyan.net

I Saw a Woman Murdered the Other Day by William Borden. Copyright © 2004 by William Borden. All rights reserved. No performance or reading of this work may be given without express permission of the author. Inquiries regarding rights should be addressed to the author at 7996 S. FM 548, Royse City, TX 75189. Email: wborden@paulbunyan.net

Credits

Looking Through You by Max Bush. Copyright © 2004 by Max Bush. Reprinted here by special arrangement of the author. All questions regarding performance royalties should be directed to Max Bush, 5372 132nd Avenue, Hamilton, Michigan 49419. Email: Maxb@egl.net

Markers by Shirley King. Copyright © 2004 by Shirley King. All rights reserved. No performance or reading of this work may be given without express permission of the author. Inquiries regarding rights should be addressed to the author at P.O. Box 1034, Benicia, CA 94510. Email: sak934@aol.com

The Minotaur by Neil Duffield. Copyright © 2003 by Neil Duffield. All rights reserved. Reprinted by permission. Information concerning rights should be addressed to the author: Neil Duffield, 2 Gorses Mount, Darcy Lever, Bolton BL2 1PQ, UNITED KINGDOM

No Pain, No Gain by Susan Battye. Copyright © 2004 by Susan Battye. All inquiries regarding performance rights and licensing should be directed to Playmarket, P.O. Box 9767, Wellington, New Zealand. Phone: +0064 4 382 8462. Email: info@playmarket.org.nz

"On Guard" by Marilyn Rofsky, from *She of the Lovely Ankle* by Women At Play. Copyright © 2003 by Women At Play. All rights reserved. Reprinted by permission of the author. Inquiries regarding rights should be addressed to Katherine H. Burkman at 2990 Shadywood Rd., Columbus, OH 43221.

Pancake Tuesday by Lindsay Price. Copyright © 2003 by Lindsay Price, all rights reserved. Reprinted by permission. Information concerning rights should be addressed to the author at 2873 Dundas Street West #302, Toronto, Ontario M6P 1Y9, CANADA. Email: lindsay@theatrefolk.com

Reconciliation by Cary Pepper. Copyright © 2003 by Cary Pepper. All rights reserved. Reprinted by permission. Information concerning rights should be addressed by email to the author: CaryPepper@aol.com

Red Frogs by Ruth Margraff. Copyright © 2002 by Ruth Margraff. Reprinted by permission of Helen Merrill Ltd. on behalf of the author. All inquiries regarding rights should be addressed to Morgan Jenness, Helen Merrill Ltd., 295 Lafayette St. Suite 915, New York, NY 10012. Professionals and amateurs are hereby warned that performances of *Red Frogs* are subject to a royalty. It is fully protected under the copyright laws of the United States of America, and of all countries covered by the International Copyright Union (including the Dominion of Canada and the rest of the British Commonwealth), and of all countries covered by the Pan-American Copyright Convention and the Universal Copyright Convention, and of all countries with which the United States has reciprocal copyright relations. All rights, including professional, amateur, motion picture, recitation, lecturing, public reading, radio broadcasting, television, video or sound taping, all other forms of mechanical or electronic reproductions, such as information storage and retrieval systems, and photocopying, and the rights of translation into foreign languages, are strictly reserved. Particular emphasis is laid upon the question of readings, permission for which must be secured from the author's agent in writing. *Red Frogs* premiered at P.S. 122 (Mark Russell, Executive Director) in February 2002, co-produced by Hourglass Group and was originally commissioned by P.S. 122 with funds provided by the Jerome Foundation and the Lower Manhattan Cultural Council.

Reliable Junk by Ric Averill. Copyright © 1997 by Ric Averill. All rights reserved. No performance or reading of this work may be given without express permission of the author. Inquiries regarding rights should be addressed to the author at 2 Winona Avenue, Lawrence, KS 66046.

Saints and Angels by Shirley King. Copyright © 2004 by Shirley King. All rights reserved. No performance or reading of this work may be given without express permission of the author. Inquiries regarding rights should be addressed to the author at P.O. Box 1034, Benicia, CA 94510. Email: sak934@aol.com

"Sam" by Katherine Burkman, from *She of the Lovely Ankle,* by Women At Play. Copyright © 2003 by Women at Play. All rights reserved. Reprinted by permission of the author. Inquiries regarding rights should be addressed to Katherine H. Burkman at 2990 Shadywood Rd., Columbus, OH 43221.

Surfing, Carmarthen Bay by Roger Williams. Copyright © 1998 by Roger Williams. All rights reserved. Reprinted by permission. Information concerning rights should be addressed to the author: c/o Drama Association of Wales, The Old Library, Singleton Rd., Splott, Cardiff CF24 2ET, Wales, UNITED KINGDOM.

Tagged by Susan Battye. Copyright © 2004 by Susan Battye. All inquiries regarding performance rights and licensing should be directed to Playmarket, P.O. Box 9767, Wellington, New Zealand. Phone: +0064 4 382 8462. E-mail: info@playmarket.org.nz

Terrestrial and Without Imagination by Luiza Carol. © 2003 by Luiza Carol. All rights reserved. Reprinted by permission. Information concerning rights should be addressed to the author: POB 1083, Kiriat-Yam 29000, ISRAEL. Email: luizac@012.net.il

The Trees They Grow So High by Tony Powell. Copyright © 1998 by Tony Powell. All rights reserved. Reprinted by permission. Information concerning rights should be addressed to the author: c/o Drama Association of Wales, The Old Library, Singleton Rd., Splott, Cardiff CF24 2ET, Wales, UNITED KINGDOM.

Two Loves and a Creature by Gustavo Ott, translated by Heather McKay. Copyright © 2001 by Gustavo Ott. All rights reserved. Reprinted by permission. Information concerning rights should be addressed to the author: Gustavo Ott, 5093 White Pine Circle NE, St. Petersburg, FL 33703-3139. E-mail: tsmcmckayott@eldish.net or gustavot@yahoo.com. Website: www.gustavoott.com.ar

Credits

Victor by Ric Averill. Adapted from *Frankenstein* by Mary Shelley, and commissioned by the Coterie Theatre, September 2002. Copyright ©2002 by Ric Averill. All rights reserved. Reprinted by permission. Information concerning rights should be addressed to the author at 2 Winona Avenue, Lawrence, KS 66046.

Wait Wait Bo Bait by Lindsay Price. Copyright © 2003 by Lindsay Price. All rights reserved. Reprinted by permission. Information concerning rights should be addressed to the author at 2873 Dundas Street West #302, Toronto, Ontario M6P 1Y9, CANADA. E-mail: lindsay@theatrefolk.com

Went Down to the Crossroads by Philip Goulding. Copyright © 2001 by Philip Goulding. All rights reserved. Reprinted by permission. Information concerning rights should be addressed to the author. Email: GouldingP@aol.com

Women Behind the Walls by Claire Braz-Valentine. Copyright © 2003 by Claire Braz-Valentine. All rights reserved. Reprinted by permission. Information concerning rights should be addressed to the author: Email: CBrazvalen@aol.com

Your Molotov Kisses by Gustavo Ott, translated by Heather McKay. Copyright ©2002 by Gustavo Ott. All rights reserved. Reprinted by permission. Information concerning rights should be addressed to the author: Gustavo Ott, 5093 White Pine Circle NE, St. Petersburg, FL 33703-3139. Email: tsmcmckayott@eldish.net or gustavot@yahoo.com. Website: www.gustavoott.com.ar

About the Editor

Roger Ellis is a theatre director, university professor, and author living in Michigan, U.S.A. He earned his M.A. in Theatre from the University of Santa Clara, and his Ph.D. in Dramatic Art from the University of California at Berkeley. He trained as an actor under Michael Shurtleff, Carlo Mazzone-Clementi of Dell'Arte, Robert Goldsby of the Berkeley Repertory Theatre, and James Roose-Evans of Great Britain's National Theatre. He has also spent nine seasons as an actor-director with repertory, summer stock, festival, and dinner theatres in California and Michigan, and he frequently conducts workshops on acting and auditioning skills in the Great Lakes region and abroad. He has authored or edited fourteen books for the stage, including anthologies, critical works, and acting texts. In 1991 he initiated an ethnic theatre program at Grand Valley State University in Michigan, creating guest artist residencies and presenting new international plays dealing with cultural diversity; in 1993 he established that university's Shakespeare Festival, currently the oldest and largest in Michigan; and in 1997 he established Grand Valley's annual New Plays-in-Process program, bringing national playwrights to Michigan for extended rehearsals and staged reading productions of their new work. He is currently the President of the Theatre Alliance of Michigan, editor of the international theatre journal *IDEACTION,* and a Professor of Theatre Arts at Grand Valley State University.

Order Form

Meriwether Publishing Ltd.
PO Box 7710
Colorado Springs CO 80933-7710
Phone: 800-937-5297   Fax: 719-594-9916
Website: www.meriwether.com

Please send me the following books:

_____ **New Audition Scenes and Monologs**   **$15.95**
from Contemporary Playwrights #BK-B278
edited by Roger Ellis
The best new cuttings from around the world

_____ **Audition Monologs for Student Actors**   **$15.95**
#BK-B232
edited by Roger Ellis
Selections from contemporary plays

_____ **Audition Monologs for Student**   **$15.95**
Actors II #BK-B249
edited by Roger Ellis
Selections from contemporary plays

_____ **The Complete Audition Book for**   **$17.95**
Young Actors #BK-B262
by Roger Ellis
A comprehensive guide to winning by enhancing acting skills

_____ **Scenes and Monologs from the Best**   **$15.95**
New Plays #BK-B140
edited by Roger Ellis
An anthology of new American plays

_____ **Millennium Monologs #BK-B256**   **$15.95**
edited by Gerald Lee Ratliff
95 contemporary characterizations for young actors

_____ **Young Women's Monologs from**   **$15.95**
Contemporary Plays #BK-B272
edited by Gerald Lee Ratliff
Professional auditions for aspiring actresses

These and other fine Meriwether Publishing books are available at your local bookstore or direct from the publisher. Prices subject to change without notice. Check our website or call for current prices.

Name: _____

Organization name: _____

Address: _____

City: _____ State: _____

Zip: _____ Phone: _____

❑ Check enclosed
❑ Visa / MasterCard / Discover # _____

Signature: _____ Expiration date: _____
(required for credit card orders)

Colorado residents: Please add 3% sales tax.
Shipping: Include $3.95 for the first book and 75¢ for each additional book ordered.

❑ *Please send me a copy of your complete catalog of books and plays.*